CELLS FOR LIFE

D1464821

Cells for Life

RON TRUDINGER

KINGSWAY PUBLICATIONS
EASTBOURNE

Copyright © Ron Trudinger 1979, 1983

First published by the Olive Tree Publications 1979

This edition 1983

All rights reserved.
No part of this publication may be reproduced or
transmitted in any form or by any means, electronic
or mechanical, including photocopy, recording, or any
information storage and retrieval system, without
permission in writing from the publisher.

ISBN 0 86065 234 3

Unless otherwise indicated, Scripture quotations
are from the New American Standard Bible,
© The Lockman Foundation 1960, 1962, 1963,
1968, 1971, 1972, 1973.

Front cover photo by James Bell,
courtesy of Science Photo Library

KINGSWAY PUBLICATIONS LTD
Lottbridge Drove, Eastbourne, E. Sussex BN23 6NT.
Typeset by Nuprint Services Ltd, Harpenden, Herts.
Printed and bound in Great Britain
by Collins, Glasgow.

Contents

Acknowledgements

I would like to express my thanks to those who have helped me in writing this book, especially to Mike Hollow for his very patient and thorough help in checking every chapter and correcting various drafts; to my wife Sue for patiently typing all those drafts over several months, and to Vic Gledhill, Tony Gray and other colleagues in Basingstoke for their advice and suggestions.

Foreword

Ron Trudinger is a sixty-four-year-old, six-foot, twelve-stone bundle of inexhaustible Australian energy. He came into my life in the spring of 1973, while I was pastoring Basingstoke Baptist Church. A total stranger to everyone, he took his place among us in an unassuming yet cheerful manner. Although he was a man of considerable scholarship no-one would have known—he was so natural, and seemed quite happy simply to enjoy us and the Lord. Ron and his lovely wife Sue increasingly found a special place of affection and appreciation in all our hearts.

It so happened that about this time our older young people were struggling in the doldrums. We asked Ron and Sue if they would take special responsibility for them, and within months forty-three were on their way to Israel for an unforgettable four weeks of adventure in evangelism and practical service to mentally and physically handicapped children.

The following year fifty-four journeyed to Kenya, dividing into five teams which travelled throughout the nation. They shared the gospel with thousands, but this time they also made a remarkable impact on Christians as they communicated through dance, drama and music the vision of the church being Christ's living, vibrant body expressing God's glory on this earth.

They performed a one-hour TV special on voice of

Kenya, which concluded with a Kenyan national embracing one of our young fellows, the final shot being of their two faces touching with radiant smiles, and in the background the cast together with the entire studio audience dancing before the Lord to the song 'Let's go up to Zion'. They shared Christ in schools, colleges, prisons and convents, before numerous church congregations, and at the International Charismatic Conference held in the Kenyatta Conference Centre, Nairobi. Our young people have never been the same since.

A river is enlarged through the tributaries that run into it. Ron and Sue ran into our river in God at Basingstoke and as a result we have been greatly enlarged.

Finally, one word of caution: if God speaks to you through the reading of this book, don't be like the foolish man who built upon the sand—he heard but failed to obey. Be like the wise man who built upon solid rock. Obey the voice of the Lord.

BARNEY COOMBS, 1979

Introduction

In one of Gilbert and Sullivan's operettas, 'Ruddigore', there is in Act Two an interesting passage in a dialogue between Mad Margaret and Sir Despard, who is a Wicked Baronet:

> *Margaret* . . . Shall I tell you one of poor mad Margaret's odd thoughts? . . . I sometimes think that if we could hit upon some word for you to use whenever I am about to relapse—some word that teems with hidden meaning—like 'Basingstoke'—it might recall me to my saner self.

We will probably never know quite why W. S. Gilbert selected 'Basingstoke' from all the thousands of names of towns in England. Perhaps it was for the very reason that it *doesn't* teem with hidden meaning.

But in fact, Basingstoke, where I am writing, does have special meaning for hundreds of its people. And hundreds have found normality through an experiment here—God's kind of normality.

Basingstoke is a town of about 80,000 people 50 miles south-west of London, between the capital and the port of Southampton.

After the Second World War Basingstoke was earmarked for development to accommodate 'London overspill' population. So in the sixties large numbers of predominantly young people, mostly uprooted Londoners

—displaced persons—moved into the developed areas. These high-density housing estates produced the unfortunately familiar pattern of problems—broken or seriously disturbed families, lonely housewives, 'latch-key kids', delinquent teenagers, vandalism and the rest.

In this setting the Baptist Church began to wake up to its responsibilities as 'salt' and 'light' to the world. When these Londoners began their invasion the church had a membership of about forty and its life was of a traditional pattern.

This pattern was challenged by two successive ministers with teaching on the power and reality of the Holy Spirit. And one of the major principles this same Holy Spirit revealed to the pastors and the congregation was that *people* matter. They matter as individuals both to God and to one another.

Gradually this awareness that *people* needed far more care and attention led to the establishment of home cells, or home fellowships. These cells have proved one of the most significant features of the church life.

This book is largely the fruit of this strategy which is not, of course, confined to Basingstoke, but is being adopted in many parts of the world in these days of the Holy Spirit's renewal.

1. A Dream!

'I have a dream!' cried Martin Luther King Jr in his famous speech in Washington DC.

In the fifties and sixties I too had a dream. I didn't express it in any famous speech, but it both disturbed and encouraged me for many years. With many others of evangelical persuasion I felt a profound dissatisfaction with church life as we knew it. We sensed that there must be better ways to ensure harmony, relevance and power in a church. We were aware of the enormous gap between what we read of in the Acts of the Apostles and what we saw and experienced in our churches.

In 1969 and 1970 I began travelling to various countries of the world, still searching. Early in 1973, having become intensely interested in my forbears, the Moravians (see Chapter 6), I planned to come to England to do some doctoral research into their missionary methods. But underlying this ostensible reason for coming here was the conviction that somehow, somewhere, I would find a fulfilment of my dream—a church community where everyone was committed and where New Testament patterns were evident, especially in relationships. I prayed that God would lead our family to such a church and I was prepared to be for a while something I had previously abhorred, a 'spiritual gypsy', so that I could find a true church 'home'.

God answered prayer rather quickly. I had never heard of Basingstoke, yet less than eighteen hours after arrival in England we found ourselves in the Baptist Church here, and slowly but surely we began to take root. My dream was becoming fulfilled.

I soon realized this was not a church where I could only be involved on a Sunday. It was a church in which relationships extended far beyond the weekly meetings and outside the walls of the church building. The people were able to deepen their relationships and their commitment to each other by gathering in home fellowships. Since then this activity has grown widely in richness and scope. If you were to ask me when and where this cell life goes on, I would say, 'Every day of the week and all around the town.'

Let's say it is Tuesday evening. Tonight in a home in a nearby village called Tadley, you would hear an hour or so of sharing of up-to-date experiences of God. This evening is being co-ordinated by Tony, an electrical engineer. This might be followed by a thirty-minute study by Tony or one of the members on, say, 'How to learn to rule your own spirit.' In another home on the same night a group would be sitting together in a shared meal and taking 'the cup after supper', remembering Jesus and the cross in loving communion. In another home tonight Howard, a male psychiatric nurse, is chairing a lively discussion on neighbourhood evangelism.

In another more outlying area, on Wednesday, the twenty or so members are regrouping in John's farmhouse after a mutually agreed day of fasting; their main purpose this night is to get to grips with God and to come against the enemy in praying for a specially poignant case of sickness in their locality.

In another home lounge on Thursday evening you could come and share in, say, the second of a Bible study series on 'Christian Hospitality'. Then you could call on a group who are for the moment sitting in virtual silence, all writing, trying their hands at creative poetry or prose—as did King David!—for the glory of God and to build one another up—and having a few hearty laughs along the way.

There are about forty such home cells in the area covered by the Basingstoke Community Church—as it is now called. The members of each local group, who normally also see quite a lot of each other during the week, come together this and most other weeks of the year on the various housing estates and in the villages in and around Basingstoke. The participants are committed Christians, members of the Community Church who now gather together on Sundays in seven local areas, and once a month for celebration in a large school auditorium in Basingstoke. These gatherings are for corporate praise and worship, teaching and just meeting up with one another.

The subdivision into small groups during the week may be seen as the 'cellular' structure of the larger body and the groups, or cells, as the place where the primary life activity of the local church goes on. Indeed these cells are the very basis of, and the key to, the corporate Spirit life and growth of its four hundred or so committed adult members. It is largely through this cell life that they mature as disciples of Jesus Christ.

As has already been indicated, the home cells do not follow any rigid formal pattern. They are not merely another example of the traditional week-night prayer meetings or Bible studies, although naturally prayer and Bible study are frequently part of the various programmes.

Watching these people, you might be surprised at the range and variety of their activities. This is because they are people learning to relate to one another in depth in all areas of life, and their time together is a most important part of life in the church, where 'all are Christ's body and individually members of it' (1 Cor 12:27) and where 'the whole body is being fitted and held together by that which every joint supplies, according to the proper working of each individual and part...for the building up of itself in love' (Eph 4:16). And real life is, or should be, full of variety and interest and fulfilment.

So you would find unpredictability and individuality in each home cell group. But there are common denominators, too.

Everything is led and with purpose; all are relaxed, enjoying one another and enjoying God—praying, studying, sharing, encouraging, learning, becoming integrated. Each cell is living and growing in its own area and within its own walls, but each is also a part of a larger organism, the local church. But are we right to call them 'cells'?

2. Cells?

A cell, in the primary sense of the word, is a biological unit. In tracing similarities between house cells and biological cells we can discover a fascinating revelation of the consistency in the mind of the Creator, our Father God.

The principles of structure and growth in normal cell life in nature are in many respects the same as those of structure and growth in the 'cells' which make up the body of Christ.

Further on we will take note of a few of the more recent discoveries about biological cells. But first let us examine in some detail the biblical origins of small group fellowships, and the significance of these in understanding God's purposes for his church today.

You may be already in a church which is subdivided into home cells. If so, it should be valuable for you to understand further the foundations and purposes of this phenomenon which is the fruit of the worldwide renewal in the Holy Spirit.

But more especially, if you are a leader or a pastor or a member of a church where this has not yet come about, it is to be hoped that this book will not only challenge you to do something about it, but will also suggest steps that can be taken and principles to be followed.

You may wonder what basis this kind of subdivision has in Scripture. Is it just a modern experiment in church life?

Or you may ask, 'How could we possibly introduce it into our church, with its long-established traditions?'

You may even have tried doing it, but found that the 'cells' petered out. This was my experience for several years. It was not until recent years that I realized what was missing in those earlier home groups.

This study, then, could well change your thinking concerning the bases and the goal of house cells—and the methods, programmes, leadership and other factors necessary for their successful functioning. We shall examine guidelines for planning divisions into home cells, details of how they operate, and pitfalls to be avoided in putting them into practice, with illustrations from our church here in Basingstoke.

Indeed, it is important to point out here that the whole of this survey is based on the experience of years in our church, and in churches elsewhere. We are not propounding a new idea or gimmick. It is not the current 'in' thing. Nor is it merely an interesting theoretical possibility based on some new 'revelation' from the Bible.

We believe with all our hearts that division into home cells is a very important part of God's plan to restore his church in the world in these days. It is relevant, up-to-date and psychologically sound. It has all the characteristics of a living, growing organism—in refreshing contrast to much of the sterility of today's organizations.

We've watched it work in churches of, say, thirty committed members, and it has been successful in at least one 'local church' (in Korea) numbering over 100,000 members, subdivided into thousands of home cells!

So read on. The home cell concept can be put into operation wherever there are local groups of genuinely committed disciples of the Lord Jesus Christ.

You don't need large numbers to start. Small is beautiful!

Also, in case you doubt it, it is for churches of any size.

3. Church and Cells

Since we are considering home cells and subdivisions of the local church, let us first look into what the 'church' is in the Scriptures. There we find several important words which describe aspects of God's ideal for his community of people called the church. I will be using these words frequently in this book as they are essential to an understanding of home cell practice. One of these words, or concepts, is *koinonia*.

Koinonia

This is a beautiful New Testament Greek word meaning fellowship, sharing, mutual communication, communion, participation. It is derived from *koinonos* which is translated partner, companion, partaker, sharer. For example, Peter uses this word when he writes '...that you might become *partakers* of the divine nature.' We must rid our minds of the popular idea of 'fellowship' as merely a cheerful, back-slapping, social contact. True biblical fellowship is something very personal, even intimate: a full, open, warm sharing of one's life and spirit with others. In short, it's what this book is all about—a subtitle, if you like—true Koinonia.

Biblical *koinonia* lies at the very core of the real nature of the church. But the real nature of the church as we see it in the New Testament is something many thousands of Christians round the world seem to know little or nothing about. The church needs a restoration. What exactly does this *restoration* mean?

Restoration

Pentecost was the first page of a new chapter in God's dealings with his 'New Covenant' people. And so it is with many thousands today. The early signs and results are similar.

There's a release into new dimensions of praise and worship.

Our tongues break into new languages, interpretation, prophecies, words of knowledge and other charismata, or Spirit gifts.

There is almost always more excitement and joy.

Jesus becomes more real. We become conscious of new revelation; scales are lifted from our spiritual eyes and we are aware of a fresh vitality, reality and power in our lives.

If we remain content, however, with these manifestations as the main outcome of the work of the Holy Ghost, we miss ninety-five per cent of the New Testament teaching. Renewal of this kind isn't the end; it's the beginning. It is our introduction to, or our initial preparation for, God's purposes for us as individuals and as churches—indeed for what he wants for his whole church on the earth. We miss out on these greater purposes if we merely continue to ride, so to speak, on a charismatic roundabout, trying to maintain the glow without learning of, and entering into, God's wider plan—the very reason for which the Holy Spirit was sent.

Renewal then is a basis for something far greater, viz. *restoration*. This is a biblical term. Peter, preaching to the crowds who gathered after the 'Beautiful Gate' healing miracle, speaks of 'the period of *restoration* of all things about which God spoke by the mouth of His Holy prophets from ancient times . . . and . . . all the prophets . . . announced these days.' Note: *these days.*

Another significant biblical reference to restoration is found in Acts 15 where James gives his judgement on a key issue, the acceptance and treatment of Gentiles in the church. After 'much debate'. James quotes Amos and says 'I will rebuild the tabernacle of David...and I will *restore* it, in order that the rest of mankind may seek the Lord.'

There are three main words in Scripture for 'restore':

Shub (Heb): to cause to turn back
shalam (Heb): to complete or make whole
anorthoo (Gk): to make straight or set right.

A dictionary definition is: to bring back as near as possible to original form. God wants to bring us, his people, the church, back to his pattern and principles to complete or mature us in his likeness.

So it is not enough to be renewed in praise, reality and joy, and then to institute and perpetuate yet another issue of man-made structures and patterns. We are clearly called to 'turn back' to the scriptural principles of church goals and structure for real growth and effectiveness. What then is the scriptural meaning of the word *church?*

Church—Ekklesia

The Greek New Testament has only one word translated *church.* Its original meaning is clear and simple, despite the confusing secondary meanings given to it over the centuries.

Although it is not obvious, the word translated *church*

is related to our word *call*.

Let's look at it this way (if you can forgive a little technical word-building). Reduce *call* to a phonetic form and we have *kal*. This in fact is the Greek root for *call*. The verb is *kal-eo*, to call. Add *ek*, like the Latin *ex*, for 'out', and we have *ek-kaleo*, to 'call out'. Give it a Greek ending for a collective noun and we have *ek-kalesia* or 'called-out ones'. The first 'a' is elided in normal speech and writing, so we have *ekklesia*, a group of called-out or chosen people.

Ekklesia occurs 115 times in the New Testament and is translated *assembly* three times, and *church* 112 times.

There are several clear deductions from this.

People
Ekklesia refers to people; it's a collective term meaning a group of people.

Not a building
The church is never a building. No record exists in the Bible or even in the first two centuries of the Christian era that a building was called a church. Indeed we don't read that Christians ever met then in places especially built for Christian meetings or services.

I suppose most of us know this, yet many seem to remain content with a sub-scriptural concept, calling the building the church.

Koinonia—not a preaching centre
Even more important: the building aspect wouldn't matter so much if in each so-called 'church' building a true *ekklesia* existed, and *ekklesia* principles applied. Many have tended to equate 'going to church' with attending what is little more than a preaching centre. They meet once or twice a week to take some small part in a structured

service and hear a preacher. Others go weekly to services where the preaching isn't the main thing, but where they take part together in a time-honoured ritual of singing, responding, reading or reciting, kneeling and standing. The question is, is there real community among them, a real practical belonging to one another in the Holy Spirit? There may be, of course. But the fact remains that the restoration of anything like real *koinonia* in a group of God's called-out, chosen ones, an *ekklesia,* is virtually unknown to millions of 'church' adherents today.

We need then to look a little more closely into the usage of *ekklesia* in the Bible.

Threefold church

An analysis of all the 112 occurrences of *ekklesia,* translated *church* in the New Testament, shows that they may be divided into three categories.

    A. The church of Jesus Christ universal
    B. The church identified with a city or town
    C. The church in a home

A. The universal church

This is what Jesus referred to when he said to Peter, 'Upon this rock I will build My church.' Quite obviously he wasn't localizing it here. He meant all the called-out, the saved ones of the earth.

Paul has a similar universal meaning in his mind when he writes to the Ephesians that 'God gave Him (Jesus) as head over all things to the church which is His body.' And further on: '...that the manifold wisdom of God might be now made known through the church to the rulers and authorities in the heavenly places.'

B. The city church

On nearly a hundred occasions *ekklesia* refers to a city or town church. For example, seven of these are city churches referred to in the celebrated words of Jesus and the Spirit to the churches in the first three chapters of Revelation: for example, 'Unto the angel of the church in Thyatira write....'

In Acts 11 we read: 'News reached the church at Jerusalem.' In Acts 20, 'from Miletus he (Paul) sent to Ephesus and called to him the elders of the church.' There are many other examples.

We never read of the church of Asia, or of Greece, that is, of any sort of national church. It is always the church of a city or town.

We can glean from historical records that some of these towns or cities were large. Paul spent a long time founding and building city churches in such places: eighteen months at Corinth and three years at Ephesus, which, for example, was a city of about 200,000. So it is clear that in some instances at least, the city church would have been far too large to meet in any one building. It had to be subdivided into smaller units.

Incidentally, the identity and the unity of a sub-divided city church would seem to have been maintained by some meeting of its leaders. When Paul called for the Ephesian elders, there must have been close communication between them all, as they appear to have assembled quickly enough. Paul addressed them as belonging to a single unit: 'Be on guard for yourselves and *for all the flock*' and 'shepherd the church of God.'

But where did the rank and file meet? Earlier, Luke referred to Paul's daily discussions in 'the lecture room of Tyrannus'. However, there is a lot of evidence that believers, during those early centuries, met in private homes.

C. The church in the home

The second chapter of Acts describes what is the beginning of New Testament church life and structure. Thousands 'from every nation under heaven' heard Peter's first sermon and responded. On the very first day of the out-pouring of the Holy Spirit, three thousand were baptized in water and added to the small group of Jesus' disciples.

Immediately, we read, they initiated the practice of meeting daily in the temple at Jerusalem—there was only one Jewish temple—and of breaking bread 'from house to house'. This term can also be rendered: 'in the various private homes'. In Acts 5:42 we read that 'every day, in the temple and *in the various private homes,* (marg.) they kept right on teaching and preaching...'

Soon after this the opposition of the orthodox Jews prevented the use of the temple. Synagogues were used for a while, but as we see in Acts 19 it was not long before many of these also were closed to Christians. But we continue to find significant references in Acts and the Epistles to churches in homes.

When for example, in Acts 12, Herod began to arrest some who belonged to the church, and then seized and jailed Peter, we read that 'prayer was being made fervently by the church' (v.5). Where? Certainly not on any church premises. It was in the home of Mary, the mother of Mark. There it was that many were gathered together praying.

Then, on the occasion of the Miletus beach assemblage of elders referred to above, Paul reminded these men that he had taught for three years publicly and 'in the various private homes'.

In the last chapter of his letter to the Romans Paul writes: 'Greet Prisca and Aquila... also greet the church that is in their house...' Elsewhere he mentions the church in Nympha's (or Nymphas', as some manuscripts read) house; and, when writing to Philemon, 'the church in your house'.

Most of us remember with sympathy Eutychus' dropping off to sleep during Paul's long preaching and falling from the window sill of the third-floor room where the local church was meeting. This seems to have been a private home.

Turning to the gospels, we find that although Jesus himself taught and preached in synagogues, in the temple and in the open air, he favoured private houses for much of his ministry. Such home occasions resulted, in the case of Zacchaeus, in the winning of the whole household to God. Also he frequently used homes for teaching and explanation, e.g. in Matthew 13:36: 'He left the multitudes and went into the house, and His disciples came . . . saying "explain to us the parable of the tares of the field". . . .'

Jesus' healing also was often in homes, as in the instance when four men let down the paralytic through the roof.

Moreover, when Jesus commissioned his twelve apostles (Mt 10), he sent them out to preach, heal, raise the dead and cast out demons. In every city and village they were to 'enter the house', implying that the private home was to be the focus of their ministry. Similarly (in Luke 10) he bade them 'enter houses', first saying: 'Peace be to this house'.

The point I wish to make is that Jesus ministered in ordinary, everyday places and didn't build, or even suggest the necessity to build, special centres or headquarters.

So it seems clear that for Jesus and the early church, the home was a normal setting for prayer, teaching, worship and fellowship. In some smaller places such as Troas, it may have been that the whole complement of the church could meet in one home. But this was obviously impossible in the case of 'all who were beloved of God in Rome' where we know there were thousands of Christians even in Paul's lifetime. Here no doubt, public halls were used for larger gatherings, while the basic meeting places remained the homes already mentioned, such as that of Aquila and Prisca.

The main point to grasp is that the Bible speaks of only two localized groupings of the church universal: the city church and the church in the home. In the *History of Christianity* (Lion) it is stated quite categorically that the earliest Christians had no special buildings, but met in private houses.

Justin Martyr (100–165A.D.), as recorded in *The Martyrdom of the Holy Martyrs,* was asked by Rusticus the prefect: 'Where do you assemble?' Justin said: 'Where each one chooses and can, for do you fancy that we all meet in the very same place? Not so: because the God of the Christians is not circumscribed by place.'

The small group for discipling

More important, however, than the nature of the meeting place is the concept of the group as a unit in which disciples can be nurtured.

Jesus did not say: 'Go into all the world and make converts,' but 'Go into all the world and make *disciples.*'

The setting for the development of true discipleship as we see it worked out in the New Testament is not in large numbers. The making of a disciple is a costly, personal process, feasible only in small groupings where the right kind of attention can be given.

As we shall now see, there is a weight of evidence in the Scriptures, borne out by commonsense and experience, that small cells of people are a logical, divine principle for growth and maturity in any local corporate grouping of God's people.

Indeed, it seems to be a clear premise in the mind of the

creator that if any organism is to be sound, it must be made up of basic units or cells which are themselves sound.

4. Biological Cells

All living matter from the simplest amoeba through all vegetable and animal life up to human life is founded on cell structure. Or to put it another way: there is nothing alive in all nature which is not composed of living cells, the very 'fabric of all life'.

It is only in the last few decades that many of the details and integral parts of each tiny cell have been positively identified, and even photographed, through modern sophisticated microscopy procedures.

I believe some of these discoveries are fascinating in view of their amazing parallel with church home cell principles. They also serve to teach and confirm much that we are experiencing in establishing and maintaining home cell structure.

So we make a brief incursion into the realm of scientific discovery and look at eight features of biological cell structure.

Miniatures

Each biological cell moves, grows, reacts, protects and reproduces as a tiny miniature of the larger body. Around each cell is a wall, enclosing the component parts in a kind of tiny room. Each cell moves, not in a slow or jelly-like fashion, but in a constant state of vitality and activity—

'fully and vibrantly alive', in the scientists' words.

We shall see that it is much the same with the church home cells. Each cell is a kind of mini-church contributing to the life of the larger congregation.

Diversity

An astounding diversity in shape, structure and function has been discovered. Cells come shaped like rods, spirals, shoe boxes, rectangles, spheres, daisies, snowflakes, runner beans and even blobs of jelly, to mention but a few. Diversity and flexibility in home cells is certainly a key to the maintenance of interest and healthy growth, as we shall see.

Nucleus

At the heart of each cell is a control or authority centre. It is the *nucleus* which, we are told, ensures *'order and survival'*. As well as ruling, the nucleus contains the blueprint for continuation of the organism for succeeding generations. Right leadership and spiritual authority in home cells is vital, and we will be looking at these aspects, as well as ways of ensuring, under the right direction, the growth and maintenance of the church.

Community

Cells in nature depend for their existence on a 'highly integrated *community life*' (the scientists' own description) within themselves and with other cells. Within each tiny cell are many parts, each one going about its business but needing materials and nourishment. These are provided by what the scientists call 'ER' which are networks carrying materials from one part of the cell to others. So there is in a normal cell complete interdependence (see Chapter 10) of each part upon the others.

Outreach

One part of cell structure which both fascinates and amuses me is the *Golgi Complex*. This consists of a few flat discs which are found in all cells. Their task is to prepare the nutriment produced in each cell in such a way that it can be distributed outside the cell—to bless others, we may say. They are named after the Italian scientist who discovered them in—of all places—the brain cells of barn owls!

No home cell exists just for itself or its own church. A home fellowship has a ministry to those around its neighbourhood.

Reproduction

Each cell has the capacity to grow and reproduce itself. This process is, simply, to divide into two other cells—a transformation which in the case of most cells is called *mitosis*. It is described as quite a dramatic process: the nucleus seems to receive a message to divide. At this, normal cell activity appears to be temporarily halted—as if in response to a signal. Then the nucleus begins to lose its normal appearance—and before long it has divided into two nuclei, and eventually we have two new cells each starting to work at full production again, each under the direction of a new command.

So, in the church, we are increasingly learning that God's arithmetic is *multiplication by division*. God's leadership 'divides' and 'multiplies'. It reproduces itself through training and discipling of others. And the home cells multiply by dividing into two.

Protection

Lysosomes in every cell have a protective and healing function—particularly in rehabilitating ailing tissues, and combating enemy inroads. It seems that one of the worst enemies of cells are viruses which make direct attacks on cell structure and components. Most cells quickly produce antibodies to fight these assaults. One of the major functions of home cell groups is warfare against, and protection from, the attacks of Satan—see Chapter 19 below.

Individuality

All cells have these common denominators in structure, but within each is 'a rugged *individuality* which can go on a rampage and break laws'—as cancer cells do. We shall be looking in some detail, later, at the dangers of independence in home cell operation.

Let us sum up these few details of biological cell structure. In each normal cell—and there are about sixty billion in each human body—the outstanding characteristics are order and authority coexisting with individualism and a wealth of variety designed to give interest and beauty to all living creation. Within each cell, moreover, is a miniature community and an active principle of interdependence: each part helping and serving others, both within and outside the cell wall. We can only stand in awe of such a Creator—and be excited at the realization that in his plan for the church, the organism he calls the body of his Son, there is similar order, breadth of function, and infinite variety, and above all community, *koinonia*.

One further important deduction from our glance at natural cells and organisms: if the cells are healthy, the organism is healthy. We are discovering that a church's health, stability and expansion depend on the real *koinonia* of its component home cells.

How big (or small) will these home cells be? Let's look at the question of numbers of people in each cell.

5. Small is Beautiful—
Ten to Twelve

There is a lovely consistency about our God and his ways as we follow them in the Bible. Nothing is done by chance. When we go right back to the original family which was to form the basis for God's chosen people (his original 'church') we find *twelve* sons of Jacob. We also find interestingly enough that Abraham's first son by Hagar, Ishmael, was promised twelve sons: 'He shall become the father of twelve princes, and I will make him a great nation.' Groups of this approximate size are found throughout Scripture.

We can trace in both Old and New Testaments a definite trend towards breakdown into small groupings for the effective care and instruction of individuals.

Take Moses for example, the first leader of that original church. How did Moses govern his *ekklesia* in the wilderness, as Stephen in the Acts calls it?

It was a very big congregation of people. We are told in Exodus 38:26 that the number of men 'from twenty years old and upward' was 603,550. When we add children, teenagers and women, the total comes to about three million souls.

Moses could well have worn himself out governing this multitude.

In fact, he nearly did.

He cried out to the people 'How can I alone bear the

load and burden of you and your strife?'

But God spoke to him through Jethro, his father-in-law, and the fundamental principle of rule, counsel and care in God's communities was there laid down—a principle of delegation of authority. We read about this in Exodus 18.

It's worth quoting in full Jethro's advice:

> You be the people's representative before God, and you bring the disputes to God, then teach them the statutes and the laws, and make known to them the way in which they are to do. Furthermore you shall select out of all the people able men who fear God, men of truth who hate dishonest gain; and you shall place these over them, as leaders of thousands, leaders of hundreds (Heb: *mayot* for a group of one hundred) leaders of fifties [*chameshem*] and leaders of tens [*asarot*] and let them judge the people at all times.

So ten was the basic grouping. It's interesting to speculate here how many leaders would have been involved. If we divide 600,000 men—assuming the *asarot*, the group of ten, referred to men as heads of families and thus to family units—by ten, we get sixty thousand small groups. Each one was led, ideally, by a God-fearing, trustworthy leader.

If we add up all the leaders who were appointed under Moses (see Deuteronomy 1:15) we have:

      600 leaders of thousands
    6,000 leaders of hundreds
   12,000 leaders of fifties
   60,000 leaders of tens

This makes up a total of 78,600 leaders. Quite an eldership for that church!

Coming over to the New Testament we find Jesus spending most of his time with twelve men (Mk 3:14). This number was no arbitrary one; we read in Luke 6 that he spent a whole night in prayer before making his decision. Then 'he chose twelve of them.'

During his three years of public ministry Jesus spoke to many thousands and would often deal with individuals, such as Nicodemus and the woman at Jacob's well. But these were occasional encounters.

It is clear that the foundational, continuing work of discipling and maturing men was with these twelve men only.

Even his famous Sermon on the Mount was not primarily given to thousands on the hillside as we tend to assume, but to the twelve disciples—with the rest no doubt listening. The Good News Bible describes it thus: 'Jesus saw the crowds and went up a hill, where he sat down. His disciples gathered round him, and he began to teach *them.*'

In the so-called high priestly prayer recorded in John 17, the Lord Jesus speaks of having 'authority over all mankind.' Nevertheless his main emphasis in this prayer is not on the many but on the few, the 'men whom Thou gavest me out of the world.' To *them* was his name manifested; *they* received his words; he guarded *them,* sent *them,* and for *their* sakes he sanctified himself.

Clearly, Jesus didn't exclude all other disciples, the many millions who would come after. But he was laying down a divine norm. Even he, the Lord of Glory, limited the number of those he felt he could effectively nurture to twelve. These twelve were the primary recipients of his attention and teaching. The core of the church Jesus came to establish, to 'purchase with his own blood', was twelve men.

Paul the apostle seems to have followed the same small group principle. It isn't as easy to pinpoint Paul's ideal number, but when lists of disciples or companions are given by Luke the historian or by Paul himself in his letters, they number ten or so.

For example, when he was first sent out by the Antioch church (Acts 13), Barnabas was his colleague on that initial missionary journey. But we miss the picture if we bypass verse 13 in the same chapter, telling of 'Paul and his companions'. When numbers and names are given in Acts 20:21–23, Luke having joined them, at least nine are named. Similarly, nine names including Paul's own are given in Romans 16, and in Colossians 4, ten are listed as fellow workers—Paul, Timothy, Tychicus, Onesimus, Aristarchus, Mark, Jesus Justus, Epaphras, Luke and Demas.

Admittedly some of these were the ones in prison with Paul. But there is an interesting consistency about the numbers given on these different occasions. Taken alone, of course, there is nothing conclusive about them. But bearing in mind Moses, Jesus, Paul and striking examples in subsequent church history, as well as what is now worldwide practice, we do well to take ten to twelve units as a divinely laid down norm for fruitful fellowship. Incidentally, ten to twelve refers to men or units. If both single people and married couples are taken as units, a home cell group could number up to twenty or so. But we have found in practice that even twenty can be unwieldy, so we have tended to reduce the actual number of persons in the group nearer to ten or so. If it is below ten—say six or eight—it is often advisable for two such cells to meet together every few weeks to provide sufficient numbers for praise and worship. But the smaller the cell, the better the discipling.

6. The Evidence of History

I happen to be descended through my paternal grand-mother from a seventeenth-century community of believers called the Moravians. These people had an enormous influence in the world, quite out of proportion to their numbers.

Their origin can be roughly traced right back to the New Testament, so I will briefly outline this now, drawing on material from a book which I wrote about them some years ago.

There is an interesting dream reported in Acts. Paul saw a man from Macedonia (now part of Yugoslavia) begging him to come over and help them. The response was one of the first gospel thrusts into Europe. Not only did Paul go, but later Titus, one of his disciples (and ultimately a fellow apostle), went to Dalmatia.

It seems that Titus' work of establishing churches there was very successful. In this area of Europe, south and north of the Danube, a genuine and deeply spiritual succession was maintained during the centuries when institutionalism threatened to obliterate true Christianity in Europe. This succession produced reformers like Jerome of Prague and John Huss, followed by small groups of true believers whose emphasis was not on mere liturgy and orthodoxy but on a living faith in Jesus and on *koinonia,* or 'brotherly harmony' as they called it. Seeking more freedom of worship, many of these settled in Bohemia, calling themselves *unitas fratrum* or 'The Unity of the Brethren', By 'unity' they meant 'community'. In a statement at an early Synod in 1464 they wrote:

> in the Congregations we will preserve peace with all, cultivate brotherly harmony, and do all in our power to further the common well-being, and to maintain firmly the bond of brotherhood in and with and through God.

They agreed to observe Christian obedience and to accept instruction, warning, exhortation and reproof from one another in a spirit of brotherly goodwill.

Luther recognized these Bohemian Brethren as effective reformers long before his time and wrote of them in 1532:

> There hath not arisen since the times of the Apostles any men whose churches come nearer to the Apostolical.

Direct successors of these Bohemian Brethren were the well-known Moravians who were to do more to evangelize the world than any other single group in the eighteenth and nineteenth centuries. They were initially a motley group of refugees who fled to Eastern Germany, to Silesia, so that they could have greater freedom of worship. When they arrived in Germany Count von Zinzendorf gave them a tract of land on which to live as a community. This community was called Herrnhut, meaning The Watch Care, or The Watch, of the Lord. Herrnhut still exists in East Germany to this day.

Count von Zinzendorf, in many ways a man centuries ahead of his time, undertook the task of welding them together into a small but spiritually powerful community. When real reconciliation came among them they all experienced a veritable Pentecost in 1727. Such was the resultant unity and zeal that by 1737 one household alone among them, of single men numbering 20—30 at any one time, had provided fifty-six recruits for the foreign mission field!

For this mission work Zinzendorf and other leaders organized a worldwide prayer chain so that they were Moravians interceding around the world every hour of 24 hours daily on a rota basis. This global prayer meeting continued unabated for 100 years! Christendom has known nothing quite like it before or since.

Undoubtedly another key to the unique influence of the Moravian community on the world—a community never numbering more than 7,000 at their home base—was their constant attention to relationships between one another, using small groupings. Zinzendorf has been said to have added *koinonia* as a third sacrament in the church. To establish and maintain the *koinonia* he instituted sub-division into small groups, or *banden* as they called them.

These 'bands' usually consisted of eight to twelve people; they were described as 'effective expressions of both the individual and the corporate responsibility for preserving the fellowship of the . . . congregation, and they were ground-springs of evangelism.' One of the modern Moravian historians notes, when writing of the *banden*, that:

> cells . . . , after which modern Christianity is reaching in order to renew and deepen its spiritual life and unity, were commonplace in the Herrnhut economy and in the settlements which, guided by Zinzendorf, the Moravians were to organize around the world.

Banden sprang up wherever the Brethren went.

Zinzendorf was much influenced in his early years by the so-called *Pietist* movement in northern and western Europe. While the *unitas fratrum* has its roots among Catholics in eastern Europe, the Pietists emerged among

Protestants as a challenge to the 'cold dogmatic slumber' into which much of the Lutheran reformation had fallen. The core of their life was what they called the *collegia pietatis*—small gatherings of ten or so which met for worship in private homes.

Zinzendorf, influenced by the leading Pietist, August Francke, with whom he had lived, had a profound effect on the eighteenth-century revival in Britain—and especially on its main figure, John Wesley.

It was largely to the Moravians that Wesley owed not only his conversion but also his evangelistic zeal. After visiting the Moravian community in Herrnhut in 1738 he wrote:

> I would gladly have spent my life here...O when shall *this* Christianity cover the earth as the waters cover the sea?

'This world is my parish,' Wesley proclaimed, and none had exemplified a wider evangelistic call and response than the Moravians.

Travelling for many years and covering countless miles on horseback, Wesley preached to hundreds of thousands in halls and in the open air. (In Basingstoke, incidentally, his reception was hostile, and he was stoned!)

Yet when it came to the maturing or discipling of many of the converts, Wesley looked upon his 'class meetings' or 'nurture cells', as Wesleyans have called them, as the kingpin of the whole movement. His ideal number in these was about eight to twelve.

Later, in the nineteenth century, the 'Holiness' movement in North America depended for its growth and maintenance on a small group structure. Such sub-divisions were almost unknown in other American churches. This could well have been because there was so little experience of the renewal in the Holy Spirit at that time.

In much more recent years, I recall hearing Bishop Dain of Sydney, Australia, in 1962, lecturing on church growth around the world. He was considered an expert on this subject. In describing what he termed the phenomenal growth of the church in South America in the 1950s and 1960s he attributed this to two main factors. First, the emphasis on the infilling and the work of the Holy Spirit—most of the vigorous expansion was in Pentecostal churches. Secondly, the fact that in South America they adopted cell structure—many thousands of small groups meeting in private homes in countries such as Brazil and Bolivia.

Something like this was a striking, if rather short-lived, outcome of Billy Graham's 1959 Crusade in New South Wales. I was present at many of the huge meetings, including the closing one at the Sydney Show and Cricket ground which was attended by 150,000 people.

All over the State small home Bible study groups were inaugurated to follow up conversions and rededications. Unfortunately many of these home groups faded out after a year or two. I believe we had yet to learn then some fundamental Holy Spirit-imparted principles concerning goals and structure which could have ensured continuation and growth.

One of the main speakers at the Graham-organized International Congress on Evangelism in Lausanne in 1974 was Howard Snyder. In his widely-read book, *The Problem of Wineskins,* he categorically states that somewhere around ten or twelve people gathering regularly in private homes is the best way to share God's purposes for his people. He also asserts: 'The small group was the basic unit of the church's life during its first two centuries.'

Already in the sixties and seventies there has been a remarkable proliferation of such groups in many congregations around the world. We heard evidence of this when in 1977, in Basingstoke, we were visited by two pastors from South Africa. They had just spent several months on an unofficial survey of 'Restoration' churches in the South and North American continents. One of their findings was that home cells are now widespread there and becoming increasingly recognized as a basic prerequisite for growth in the local church. In most cases this was looked upon not as an optional extra, but as an essential ingredient of corporate life, an ingredient which led to both stability and expansion.

Let's look now in a little more detail at an outstanding example of this, not in America but in Korea.

The Full Gospel Central Church in Seoul is considered the largest single church in the world, numbering over a hundred thousand members, with numerous pastors, elders, and thousands of deacons. These numbers would seem to be far too unwieldy for effective handling, but pastoring or shepherding them has proved possible because of their cell subdivision.

In 1964 the head pastor suffered a breakdown from sheer exhaustion, because of the workload. Soon he and others in the church realized that plurality of leadership and delegation of authority was God's plan for them.

For the proper maturing of each committed member of that vast congregation, a series of carefully planned sub-divisions was put into effect. Seoul, a city of over seven million people, was divided into eight 'districts' which were further broken down into six to nine 'sections', each headed by a section leader.

In each section there were from twenty-five to a hundred house fellowships, 'home cell units' as they term them—a total of thousands of cells in the church (over 5,000 in 1979).

These cells each have a leader, usually with an assistant. The church considers the ideal membership of each cell to be about twelve units or households. As is the case in Basingstoke, the numbers in each cell may be slightly fewer, or more, depending on the actual number of members in any particular geographical area.

When in the Seoul church a cell grows to over fifteen or so 'units' it will divide into two—the natural pattern of cellular reproduction, as we observed earlier.

For more than eighteen years this cell structure at Seoul has not only worked, but has also proved the indispensable key in ensuring adequate care for each member of that enormous community and in stimulating outreach. Because of this, John Hurston, writing of the undertaking, sums it up thus: 'I am . . . deeply convinced that God gave us the right and needed principles when we began together . . . ' The application of these principles has resulted in the founding of three other churches in Seoul and twenty-five in other parts of Korea. These figures were given in 1979 and have increased greatly. Many missionaries, moreover, have been sent out all over Asia.

Barney Coombs was the pastor of the Basingstoke Baptist Church when home fellowship cells came into being, largely through his teaching and initiative. He wrote about their inception in an article for *Renewal* in 1975, called 'New Wineskins in Basingstoke'. Here is an excerpt from this article:

> . . . We soon found new wine cannot be corked up in a Baptist bottle and so the cork went pop. We opened our services right up for congregational participation. People gathered at the service with a glorious optimism . . . . Then a serious problem began to develop; because of greatly increased numbers, proportionately fewer people were able to take part in the meetings. I saw signs of lethargy creeping in, and so house fellowships began to come into existence.
>
> I can't describe our feelings adequately, but suffice it to say that we were strangely aware that our feet were treading on

holy ground. There was a sense of awe and indefinable antici-
pation. I realised that something was happening which was
irreversible. No longer would I be able to keep a strong hold
on the fellowship; it is true I was apprehensive—we had never
travelled this route before, but I knew we were being borne
along by God the Holy Spirit. We had begun to discover the
new wineskin. Little did we realise the implications bound up
in that discovery.

Basingstoke is neatly divided up into housing estates, so
our members were encouraged to start meeting together
during the week, with the proviso that each meeting was
restricted to those living on that estate. We still however
retained the mid-week service on the church premises. It was
at this time that God showed us we were far too meeting-
orientated and that His kingdom life had an awful lot to do
with home life, marriages, raising of children, and getting
along with the next door neighbours, as well as caring for and
sharing with the other brothers and sisters in the community.
Fellowship could not be restricted to just meetings. This new
wine required a wineskin as big as twenty-four hours a day,
seven days a week, fifty-two weeks a year. So in the summer
of 1974 we stopped our Wednesday meeting at Sarum Hill
and concentrated entirely on the estate house fellowships.
The ship was now well and truly launched...

In outlining now some goals and principles to be followed
in the establishment of home cells where *koinonia* is
paramount, let's note again: this is not just a theory or a
doctrine. We're concerned here with the divine plan of
ekklesia life and relationships; not with ecclesiastical
dogma. This scriptural plan often runs counter to traditional habits and tenets of church structure. 'Religious' or
'pious' as these may seem to be, they often have little to do
with what the New Testament describes as the body of
Christ. Paul specifically inveighs against 'delight in
religiousness' in Colossians 2:23 (margin). The chapters
which follow, in Colossians, do not describe a religious

format but a practical way of life. We can call it God's covenant life.

7. *Nature and Goals*

Home cells as we are considering them here are not merely Bible study or prayer groups. Nor are they just 'caring and sharing' groups.

This is in no way belittling Bible study or prayer. But limiting the ministry in home fellowships to only one or two aims can limit God's expanding and maturing work in each participant's life. Also the broad and varied contribution of home cells to the whole life of a church may be lost by narrowing their activity in this way.

Let me explain this more fully.

Take Bible study, for example. Of course, Bible teaching must be a major part of any local church programme. The Bible is our textbook. But a man—and we have seen this happen here in the past—may be a thorough Bible student with his head crammed with knowledge of texts, doctrines, dispensational truth, 'types' and a whole lot more, and yet be on the verge of having his wife divorce him!

Bible study by itself, vital as it is, doesn't ensure character development.

We had an example of this some time ago. A young couple came down from London and soon joined in a local fellowship group. For a while it seemed that they grew in understanding of *koinonia* principles, and were willing to come under caring leadership.

The husband spent a great deal of time in reading books and studying the Bible with the theme of what is called 'dispensational truth' in mind. As he became more and more absorbed in this, two things began to happen. First, his marriage seemed to have growing problems which he would not acknowledge. Secondly, he became increasingly critical of the whole Fellowship and all it stood for. More and more his readiness for friendship and fellowship deteriorated. The more he 'studied the Bible' the less character development was evident. Sadly, it was not long before he left the home cell and the church.

The same Lord who said 'You search the scriptures because you think that in them you have eternal life; and it is them that bear witness of Me,' also said, for example, 'If you do not forgive others, then Your Father will not forgive you either.' So a man who studies his Bible a lot but has an unforgiving spirit is in danger of missing out on God's forgiveness and of coming to a halt in his spiritual growth. Many of us are quite skilled—albeit unconsciously—in deceiving ourselves. We can spend a lot of time reading the Bible but consistently fail to obey some of its simplest and clearest precepts. We need the objective discernment of others in our character development.

On the other hand we don't seek character development in a vacuum. The character God wants in us is based on biblical principles. So there would be imbalance if a group majored almost solely in sharing and reconciliation and was ignorant of the gifts of the Spirit, or the lordship of Jesus Christ or even the nature of effective prayer, for example.

The life God means us to have as members of his community, the body of Christ, is one with many facets. It is these that determine the wide range of activity and ministry in home cells. I propose in the next chapters to outline some of the features and goals of home cell life.

Many scriptures will be referred to but for the sake of conciseness most references will be listed at the end of the book.

It is recommended, however, that you look up these passages and study them if you want to understand more fully God's pattern of a restored church.

I will also be using case histories from our experience here and elsewhere to illustrate the points made. You see, the 'nature and goals' referred to in this chapter's headings are not what cell groups are merely *supposed* to achieve. I'm writing of what we have proved, in practice, to work over quite a number of years.

8. Change

Oliver Cromwell is reputed to have asked his portrait painter to paint him 'warts and all'. Sometimes we use this phrase to illustrate the fact that Jesus accepts those who come to him just as they are, 'warts and all'.

We often forget, however, that Jesus doesn't want us to keep the warts! As the hymn writer puts it, I come to him 'just as I am', but his purpose in receiving me is not to leave me just as I am, but to transform me progressively into his likeness, which is very different. A revolutionary difference.

So transformation is the first and foremost goal of any discipling. Jesus didn't spend the three years with those twelve men just to have company. Or even just to teach them.

His purpose was to bring about *change* constantly in their lives. Change in their ambitions, faith, habits, attitudes, priorities. In short, he constantly impressed on them by word and example the necessity of revolutionary change in their character and way of life, to bring about maturity in them.

We seem to have lost this emphasis in our church life— and even in evangelism. We stress regular attendance, doctrinal soundness or 'the Lord's service' without a deep concern about whether or not a man or woman is changing for the better.

I'm not arguing here that a change in character wins a man his salvation. We are saved not by works but by grace. But the weight of New Testament teaching is that salvation must produce *change* in a person. 'If any man be in Christ he is a new creation.'

Paul prays that the Romans may be transformed by the 'renewing of their mind,' and to the Corinthians he asserts: 'we are being transformed into the same image from glory to glory.'

Nothing in the New Testament supports the idea (all too common) that a mere intellectual stance, a 'head' belief regarding Christ and the cross, is enough to save a man. Saving faith must involve a profound transformation of the spirit deep within a man: 'believe in your heart' as we read in Romans 10:9. This is followed in verse 10 by 'for with the heart man believes *resulting in righteousness.*'

True repentance and saving faith involve the obedience of our whole being to the living Lord:—the *'obedience* of faith' (Rom 16:26). This results in actual, constant changing of a person's character and life.

Such a change was never meant, surely, to be temporary. The all-too-familiar case of a man or woman enthusiastically finding Christ and subsequently showing little change or growth is a travesty of true discipleship.

Jesus never represented discipleship as being easy or shallow. However we interpret his challenge '...whoever does not carry his own cross and come after Me cannot be My disciple,' it certainly does not mean just holding certain beliefs or following a ritual and showing little change in lifestyle.

Repentance isn't just being sorry for a while and then going back to it all.

'Bring forth fruits in keeping with your repentance,' said John the Baptist—and Jesus never cancelled out this requirement. We've conveniently forgotten, many of us,

Jesus' warning: 'Unless your righteousness surpasses the righteousness of the scribes and Pharisees, you shall not enter the Kingdom of Heaven.'

Well then, how is a consistent and constant change brought about in a man's life?

Paul clearly relates change and maturity to what he calls 'building up'—to personal interaction, to *koinonia*. His word to the Galatians in chapter six of his letter may be paraphrased thus: 'My brothers, if anyone of you is caught up in some sin, you others who are of the Spirit should gently seek to restore him—being very careful of that temptation yourselves. You should bear one another's burdens and so bring to fulfilment Christ's own law.'

The body of Christ is not provided for us as some kind of club, for temporary enjoyment and inspiration. The mutual influence of each upon others, the participation of each member, is described by Paul as being specifically for the building up of one another and of the body. This 'building up' is not some ethereal influence. It's real and visible. The members know it; each one changes, develops, matures. The world can see it.

Now such close personal interaction is difficult to put into practice solely in weekly gatherings of large numbers, necessary as these are for teaching, worship, encouragement, inspiration and witness. But it is possible to work it out, week after week, month after month, in a small warm, Spirit-led home fellowship.

When Paul writes: 'We are to grow up in all aspects unto Him, who is the head, even Christ, from whom the whole Body being fitted and held together by that which *every joint supplies* according to the *proper working of each individual part,* causes the growth of the Body for the building up of itself in love,' he makes growing up dependent on the parts or members being 'fitted together'.

This verse, a key one in this study, merits very careful

re-reading. I used to read it often—I suppose for forty years—and interpret it as a pleasant theory having little day-to-day practical application.

Then I began to see it work out in hundreds of lives in scripturally constituted home cells.

Let me illustrate with an example from a community church following the principles set out in this book. (Incidentally, 'community' here is used in the sense of *koinonia*, already outlined. It does not mean 'commune' —all living under one roof or literally sharing a common purse.)

Christine came from some distance away to live in the area covered by this church. Although she was a Christian, and had experienced renewal in the Holy Spirit, she had never been part of a home cell, or even heard of this kind of fellowship. Despite her years of affiliation to churches, her many serious personal problems hadn't been touched. She had developed a defensive stance of stubbornness and pride, and no one had been able to help her or even to point out some of the things that were wrong.

Her philosophy had been: 'Jesus and I can make it,' like the old Negro spiritual: 'Just Jesus and me, we travel the road.' The trouble with this position is that it ignores the very real provision Jesus has made to enable us to 'travel the road,' namely his body, his family.

Christine had not known this, but it wasn't really her fault. No one had ever presented her with the necessity and the glorious possibility of *change*. 'Church' life had never meant this to her. Sadly, moreover, her hang-ups and guilt had produced severe bouts of depression and even a lot of ill health.

After attending the Sunday services for a few weeks Christine heard of the home fellowship group in her area, and was invited to attend. Slowly she began to participate in the cell's activities which included meals out, Saturday excursions and other outings, as well as the weekly evening gatherings. Friendships and relationships were built up over the months, quite different from what she had previously known. She was accepted and she could see that as she started to open up to others and invite prayer and counselling, her burdens were being shared by others and so became lighter.

She even welcomed helpful, loving correction of her ways. Correction not from a whole group but from chosen leaders who, she began to see, were there 'to keep watch over her soul as those that must give account,' as the writer to the Hebrews puts it.

Most important of all, Christine began to change, and to change for the better. At last Jesus' lordship in her life was beginning to be real and observable. There was a new sparkle in her eyes. Depression and illhealth gradually disappeared. Freed from 'bondage to unrighteousness' through the prayers of the group and its leader, she can now say with Tennyson:

My strength is as the strength of ten, because my heart is pure.

Not only is she stronger, but she is sweeter, and much more the real self God wants her to be. No suppression of personality here; no mere servile submission. The whole process has been a voluntary one. Through the help of other members of the body of which she is now really a part, Christine is experiencing the rewards of true discipleship.

Stories of change of this kind taking place over a few months or years could be duplicated hundreds of times in Basingstoke alone. I would like to relate one more brief case history—this time of a couple.

Colin and his wife Ellen moved here a few years ago to have a change after many years of full-time interdenominational ministry that had proved a great strain.

Friends from churches knowing something of restoration had advised Colin that it wasn't necessarily right that he wear himself out in this way, especially as it jeopardized the welfare of his wife and family as well. It was gently suggested to him that when the Spirit said: 'Husbands love your wives as Christ loves the church and gave Himself up for her,' he did not mean: 'Be so involved in Christian service that your marriage is threatened and your children suffer!'

Colin therefore settled on one of our housing estates having found a secular job with help from the members of the church. Before long he and Ellen joined the local home cell.

It is interesting to watch different people experiencing the therapy of corporate love, as we may call it. It usually takes someone a number of months to realize that his marriage, family, habits and even health can be changed radically. We evangelicals can be strangely complacent even in the midst of frustration and work-imposed pressure that make us feel like screaming. It would seem to be very much in Satan's interest to persuade us that this is normal Christian lifestyle, and to hide from us God's far, far better way for us—a way of growth towards security, serenity, fulfilment and maturity.

In the weekly setting of a small group of loving, caring, sharing, praying, honest men and women—like him, baptized in the Spirit—Colin began to feel the need for change in himself, and to sense the benefits of opening up his life to others. He approached the leader in the area and asked for personal care and pastoring, or 'shepherding', welcoming counsel and correction.

As a direct result of this he now saw that as God's appointed head of his household he needed to assume this role much more practically and effectively. Over the ensuing months he and Ellen willingly co-operated in the process of change through interaction with fellow members of the body. The result was that their relationship with each other, their health and finances, their children's welfare and upbringing, and their depth of genuine fellowship in the church all took a radical turn for the better.

In all the twelve previous years, these two had prayed, studied the Bible—and taught from it—heard sermons, and evangelized others, but any change seemed only for the worse. Now the love of Christ expressed daily and personally by the cell leaders and members is restoring and healing in a way undreamt of before. In fact, at this present time Colin and his family are preparing to be commissioned by the church here to go out as part of a pioneering community settling in another city in England to establish a kingdom restoration church there.

So if we would only understand it, salvation, *soteria* (Gk) has truly come to Colin, Ellen and their family—as *soteria* basically means soundness.

Paul must have had this year-by-year transformation very much in mind when he wrote to the saints in Philippi who, it is recorded, met on river banks and in private homes. He encouraged them to 'work out' (a plural verb, implying corporate action) their '*salvation* not as in my presence only, but much more in my absence.'

It is in the practical and realistic *koinonia* of home cell life that our salvation is made real and proves itself in radical change and growth.

9. Roots

A plant changes as it grows, but it will not grow if it is not securely rooted in the source of the right nourishment.

A habit of merely attending, hearing, contributing and conforming does not necessarily provide you with the roots which you need in order to change and to grow.

In one of Paul's celebrated prayers, he asks that the Ephesians should be 'rooted and grounded in love, to be able to comprehend with all saints what is the breadth and length and height and depth and to know the love of Christ.'

Jesus can, and sometimes does, reveal his love privately to a disciple. If, however, we take into account the many references to 'love' in the scriptures, we see that mutual love between members—horizontal love—is as important as God's love for a man and his for God—vertical love.

'If someone says, "I love God" and hates his brother, he is a liar; for the one who does not love his brother whom he has seen, cannot love God whom he has not seen,' writes John. So 'rooted and grounded in love' refers as much to our relationship with other members of the body as to our relationship with God.

Have you ever noticed that we don't read of being 'members of a church' in the New Testament, but we do read of being 'members of one another'?

We talk of being attached to such and such a church.

'Attachment' isn't what God wants. A rose bush or an apple tree is not 'attached' to the soil, nor indeed is fruit merely attached to a branch. There is deep, organic, intimate belonging.

Ted Ascot, who came to us from overseas with his family several years ago, was a Christian but a rootless one. Until he came here he had been a traditional 'church member'.

We helped to find him a house and encouraged the family to come into an active, united home cell group. Any change in Ted was a slow process, as it often is. There was a restlessness about him—not shared by his wife— which made it difficult for him to accept continuing, loving counsel and help. It seemed as though the habit of being just a 'church member' was permanently ingrained.

Long hours of friendly conversation with him seemed to have some effect. God, however, as we've learnt, doesn't push anyone further than he's willing to go. Ted was unhappy with his work, his family relationships and his Christian life, but would not really settle in the group or let anyone point out how necessary it was that he take his place as responsible head of his family.

To their dismay he decided to return overseas. In the farewell gathering other members expressed their conviction that God longed to provide this family with roots and a sense of belonging in the body of Christ. There is no question but that this man could have become 'rooted and grounded in love' in his home cell gathering if he had so chosen.

This is admittedly a disappointing story. It illustrates that the success of even a well-run home cell is limited by the response of the individual believer.

The story of Ken by contrast is much more positive. Ken had been an earnest, hard-working member of an evangelistic organization. But the impression he gave when he came into the Fellowship here was that he lacked roots. His immediate family had broken up, so Ken knew little of real belonging in natural or fellowship families. He was intense and zealous, but, in a sense, disorientated. He couldn't relax. He found it hard to understand what it meant to be filled with the Spirit and experience real *koinonia* with others.

He soon settled, however, in a home fellowship group, attended young people's conferences and asked a lot of questions. I, as well as others, spent time in explaining *koinonia* life to him. Furthermore, a special task was found for him which he has done for years now with exceptional skill and faithfulness.

Through all this personal attention and interaction Ken has experienced a Holy Spirit renewal, is now well rooted in the church and is valued for his significant contribution to its life.

'Rooted and grounded in love': this is what our involvement with one another in a church is meant to be. Nothing in the Bible encourages us to settle for anything less, such as mere 'signing on', 'being transferred to', or 'joining an organization'.

We can, of course, experience a feeling of identity with a large Christian community. We can even feel rooted in, and identified with, a whole nation. But this kind of belonging isn't radical and life-changing on a day-to-day basis.

We have found that it is in the smaller groupings—the natural families and cell group families—that being 'rooted and grounded' is truly possible.

10. Interdependence

It may surprise some to read this, but at the core of all sin and alienation from God is *independence*.

'We have turned every one into his own way' is how Isaiah describes the sin that sent Jesus to the cross. An important goal of home cells is to nurture the right kind of interdependence.

In the legends of the Far West in America the 'lone ranger', the hardy pioneer, was celebrated in story and song.

There have been thousands of Christian loners— especially in the last century or two—who have tried to 'do their own thing' in 'the Lord's service', but have failed. Others have genuinely believed they were subordinating their own desires to do God's will. But it was God's will as *they* saw it. They were not commissioned by the body of Christ.

Even in the Old Testament where there are many stories of pioneers, none were called to 'do their own thing'. In every case they were raised up by God to do his will, and, be it noted, always for the sake of a people, a community, never just for their own good.

Perhaps Moses is the outstanding example. He thought initially, at the prime age of forty, that he could act on his own initiative and start saving his oppressed people. But it took another forty years for him to become more humble, and to achieve leadership by obeying God. And, as we have already seen, he governed in plurality. When he acted independently, he was gently corrected by Jethro.

Elijah thought he was a 'loner', but the Lord quietly reminded him that he was one of seven thousand in Israel. We can be sure Elijah wouldn't have been so dejected if he had regularly shared fellowship with, say, just twelve of those seven thousand.

I have not known of anyone consistently participating in a successful home cell who is constantly lonely. 1 Corinthians 12 gives us very persuasive teaching on the way we need one another and cannot normally manage alone. It is not just sad, it is wrong to say (see v.21) 'I have no need of you' in the body of Christ.

In this connection I would like to relate a little of Betty's story. Betty came from an unhappy home. Her father was a heavy drinker, and she felt rejected as a child and as an adult. She spent eleven years as a missionary in Africa. Early in these years she broke her arm and took morphine for the pain. Unfortunately this led to drug addiction which lasted eighteen years. Some of the other missionaries tried to help her but Betty was unable to break the habit. On her return to England, feeling a complete failure, she wandered around the country for another eleven years with little or no contact with Christians. It was a terrible time for her, and she often wished for a group of people to stand with her and somehow help her to be freed.

Then, in 1970, through friends to whom she had turned in desperation, she visited Basingstoke. As she sat in that first service here she felt inexplicably moved to tears, and wondered whether God could do the impossible for her. A year later she came to see the pastor, Barney Coombs, who counselled her and arranged for her to stay with a church family.

Immediately the love and care of the pastor and people who hardly knew her was overwhelming. She had never known—in her own words—'the body functioning' as she now found it.

None of these new brothers and sisters mentioned the drug addiction in those first weeks, but they demonstrated such love and freedom that within ten days Betty stopped taking drugs and began a process of rehabilitation.

It took several years before Betty felt totally rooted and established in the Fellowship through the ministry of leaders and her involvement in home cells. She testifies now that she has never felt more secure and wanted; no more does she have to go it alone.

This interdependence does not mean that other people run our lives. We are not puppets, manipulated by other members. But in a real sense we are learning that each of us is our brother's keeper. We are specifically told to help to bear one another's burdens.

Burden bearing

Again in a large congregation this often has little meaning in the daily life of each individual member.

Let's look a little more closely at this bearing of burdens.

Jesus is, we know, the ultimate bearer of our burdens. As well as dying for us and taking on himself our sins on the cross, he invites all who are 'heavy-laden' to himself that they might find rest.

Peter echoes this invitation: 'casting all your care (or anxiety) upon Him, for He cares for you.' It is noteworthy, however, that Peter promises this in the context of a special message to elders, whom he looks upon as 'under-shepherds' shepherding their flock and being 'examples to those allotted to their charge.'

So Jesus, the great Shepherd, has provided such under-shepherds for the purpose of carrying out his care for us. He promises to bear our burdens, yes, but usually he does this through his body, the church, where the members 'bear one another's burdens'.

My burdens are not fully borne in a relevant, realistic, continual way by my hearing sermons on Sundays, or by occasional notice being taken of me when things are going wrong. But I do find that in a small, growing-together group, my problems of frustration, grief, bereavement, failure, suffering, rejection and even temptation can be shared and often solved.

Thus Jesus fulfils his promise through his body, as its members, possessing his hands, his smile, his tender understanding and his comfort, bear one another up constantly.

Encouragement

We all need this, don't we? Somehow many of us have not seen the connection between the death of Jesus and the personal encouragement of every Christian.

Jesus died and, as Paul put it, shed his blood to 'purchase the church'. And the church he died for is especially designed for encouragement. In his first Thessalonian letter Paul declares this very plainly, alluding specifically again to the cross:

> The Lord Jesus Christ died for us... that we may *live together* with Him. *Therefore encourage* one another and build up one another, just as also you are doing.

In a large congregation the individual tends to lose his or her identity. Many of us have known of young men or women with verve and vision who have left the local scene to join other organizations—albeit Christian—because they cannot find fulfilment in the local congregational structure. I'm not ruling out the value of many of these organizations, but the point is—should not each integral member be able to find identity and fulfilment in his home church? (We are not referring here to being sent out on a specific mission by the church, as Paul and Barnabas were by the Antioch church.)

In the daily and weekly interaction of members in home cells, one of the outstanding features is universal participation—everyone playing his or her part with appropriate recognition and encouragement. Paul writes 'When you assemble, *each* one has a psalm, has a teaching, has a revelation'...

Further on in this book I shall be listing numerous proved ways of participation.

When members of a smaller group really get to know one another and actively seek to involve all, barriers break down and deep needs become evident. One of the needs we all have is for acceptance and recognition. An all-too-common situation in churches is that of unmarried women. Whether or not God has marriage in view for them, each needs to feel accepted and integrated, having a significant function in the church.

A good example of such provision occurred in our community recently. Beryl had found employment here in Basingstoke after a number of years in a responsible position in a foreign country. It wasn't easy for her to settle into a home fellowship. For a group and its leader to take her under their wing and relate with her in a close and loving way every week was for her an unusual experience. She found it hard to place herself under a leader who would 'keep watch' over her soul. But hardest of all, possibly, was that after those busy years overseas she now felt unfulfilled.

Love found a way: the love of Jesus channelled through

the group of people. It took time—and it's hard to explain all the factors that break down the shells in which we can enclose ourselves. Obviously, just going to church does not normally do it.

In Beryl's case the task of writing an introductory question-and-answer Bible course for newcomers and converts was given to her. The course was very well written, and she began to have recognition. She now plays an important part in the life and growth of the church. In all the warmth of weekly home cell *koinonia* Beryl has begun to find much greater security, and to feel that she really belongs. (The above mentioned newcomers' course has now been printed for the Community Church by the Olive Tree Press and is available from the church at 48 Sarum Hill, Basingstoke. The book is entitled *First Steps*.)

11. Warning and Correction

This process of integrating in home fellowships is not all sweetness and light, of course. In the passage mentioned in the previous chapter, where Paul writes of encouragement, he also writes: 'We urge you brethren, admonish the undisciplined...'

This is an essential part of the new covenant *koinonia*, an element which is much stressed in the Bible but not practised widely today.

I am not referring here to cases of severe church discipline in exceptional circumstances. I am writing of the normal maturing process. The kind of thing the writer of the book of Proverbs constantly mentions: 'He is on the path of life who heeds instruction. But he who forsakes reproof goes astray.'

We tend to be frightened of concepts like admonishment, correction and warning. 'Surely if a man is undisciplined in his life, that's his business,' we would perhaps say. We feel that interference in such areas is unwarranted. We ask, 'Is this what the church is for?'

The answer is 'Yes'. It is part of God's dealing with us. It is part of his constant purpose which is to mature us.

Chapter 12 of Hebrews affords one of the best explanations of how and why God wants to straighten us out. The process here is called 'disciplining' or 'chastening'. It is usually unpleasant while it lasts, but it 'yields the peaceful fruits of righteousness'.

A preacher speaking to a congregation can certainly warn and admonish the people. Most of us, however, frequently need something closer and more direct. We're quite skilful at persuading ourselves that we've heard the hard words and will put them into effect, but then doing little about it. Any correction is more likely to be implemented when each of us has a leader who takes a caring but objective stance, and when we are part of a small group of people whom we know well and whose lives also are open to such correction.

Timothy is commanded to 'reprove and rebuke' with 'great patience and instruction'—which seems to indicate a long-term, painstaking care of people. Not in a domineering way: the 'Lord's *bondservant*,' (i.e. *slave*) must be 'kind to all, able to teach, patient when wronged, with gentleness correcting those who are in opposition.' 'Nor yet as lording it over those allotted to your charge,' echoes Peter.

None of us finds this sort of ministry easy, either to give or to take. But if I genuinely want to keep on course with God, daily, weekly, I want to be told when I'm deviating. In the more intimate relationships of a home fellowship, under leaders who lovingly care for me, I begin to drop my masks, my self-sufficiency—and my resistance to change.

Under this counsel and influence I not only keep on course with God, but when necessary change course with him too. I trim the sails. I throw over some ballast. I slow down or speed up. I avoid collisions or rocks. Indeed I avoid shipwreck when I make it easy for others to confront me in God, and in love, for my own welfare.

It's not inappropriate that I've adopted the first person pronoun here. In my own case I've experienced this sort of frank yet loving care and counsel over the past eight or nine years for virtually the first time in forty years of being a Christian.

An important caution has to be given here. We are not saying that correction is normally given in a cell gathering. Rebuke is not public. We never seek to embarrass one another in the group setting. But somehow my will to be constantly changed is activated or stimulated by the living example of others with whom I have intimate fellowship. I want to change because everyone is wanting to change.

Personal correction is the prerogative of a leader, or of leaders, who themselves should be equally open to similar counselling. How this works out in practice will be further illustrated in another chapter.

Does the prospect of some life-changing reproof frighten you? Let me assure you, that reproof is only one occasional aspect of discipling.

What do you really desire for your life? Do you honestly want God's will for your life? Which do you see as best for yourself or your church: sweeping the debris under the carpet year by year? Or living a life which is nourished and pruned and therefore flourishing in ever-increasing beauty and maturity? Do you want to be fruitful?

12. Fruit

This is yet another goal of home cell interaction.

What does fruitfulness in the kingdom mean? Surely it implies results, worthwhileness and effectiveness in our Christian lives. In an individual sense, fruits are described as attributes such as love, joy, peace, patience, gentleness and others. In a corporate sense, fruit—which in nature is normally meant to be eaten—should bless others. Jesus tells his disciples to 'Go and bring forth fruit.'

What I am trying to emphasize is that fruit is not just a vague, invisible, 'religious' result. It's observable. It's actual. If God is really working in a man's life, it is visible to others, and it has a positive effect on others.

The vine

Jesus gave a memorable discourse on the subject of the vine, the branches and the fruit in John 15. His condition for bearing fruit is 'abiding'. This is usually seen to refer to our personal relationship with him. Obviously this is primary.

But looking further into this passage, we find that 'abiding' is related to his words and commandments. Then directly following this are the words 'This is my commandment, that you love one another, just as I have loved you.' We might expect the main emphasis to be on our love for

Jesus or for the Father. But Jesus deliberately shifts the emphasis on to loving one another. And this is not a sentimental love. It is 'love...as I have loved you.' Well then, how did he love them? How was his love practically demonstrated?

The answer is plain in the gospels: he demonstrated his love by personally teaching, training, caring for, warning and encouraging his disciples. By undertaking even the most menial slave's task, washing their feet. In short, a constant shepherd-like attention during those three years. Giving them, his disciples—not the crowds—the better part of his time and attention.

You see, we can completely miss the strength of 'love one another', and merely mouth sentiments about fellowship and unity, if we fail to take into account the staggering breadth of that qualifying phrase '*just* as I loved You.'

We deduce then that 'abiding', i.e. remaining and growing in Christ like a branch on a vine, with the resultant fruit, is inseparably bound up with our practical relationships with each other in God's family.

Love is seen to be something greatly different from a mere feeling or verbal expression. People say 'I love everybody' when in hard fact they have no one to love. No one, in a sense, on whom to *practise* love, as Jesus practised it.

The very familiar 'fruit of the Spirit' set out in the Galatian epistle, i.e. love, gentleness, goodness and patience and others, is measured by observable attitudes to, and dealings with, other people. Indeed, these attributes are most observable and most practically worked out, I want to emphasize, in smaller groups of committed believers bonded together.

Teaching

We may be sure that this fruitfulness does not appear

automatically in home groups. There is a recurrent need, as in all church life, for teaching, and the house fellowship is one of the settings for this ministry. It's a little different from teaching imparted from the pulpit or in books.

To explain this I would like to use the analogy of the classroom and the school assembly—having spent a number of years as a teacher and headmaster.

In a school it is necessary to assemble large numbers each morning or on regular occasions. The head or other teachers will use these times for encouraging, advising, announcing, warning and even some general teaching. But in the average school, no one imagines that the learning process stops here. The place for normal daily instruction is, of course, the classroom with its smaller groupings. In fact many teachers would opt, if they had the choice, for classes reduced to say ten to fifteen in number.

The main point about the class situation is that it gives practical recognition to the truism that learning is much more than sitting and listening to words. A good class teacher knows each pupil and watches over and guides the group. He or she corrects and encourages individual pupils in a way quite impossible in the larger assembly.

In my training, years ago at a teachers' college, we learnt a very useful aphorism: 'No impression without expression.' You haven't really learnt something until you write it down, or use it, or somehow show *observably* that you know it.

The home cell is comparable with the class. It is in the local grouping normally that we find teaching really learnt and applied.

As a practical outworking of this impression-expression principle, we have sometimes adopted a general plan here in Basingstoke which works like this: the pastors of the church, who work as a team, agree on a broad thematic framework for a few months ahead. After spending time in biblical research and study, the pastor-teachers develop this theme in a series of teaching sessions—sermons, if you like—with the Sunday morning congregations. Everyone is encouraged to take notes, especially the home cell leaders.

Then, on the week night when each local group meets, room is often made for questions, discussion, illustration and expansion of what was taught on the Sunday. Thus the Bible exposition is brought right down to a day-to-day level, and each one is encouraged to put the principles taught into effect.

The above plan is our ideal. Like everything else in God's dealings with us, there is no hard and fast legality about it (unless we're dealing specifically with unrighteousness and God's standards of holiness).

There may be evenings, for example, when immediate needs do not allow for teaching. One thing is certain: in our fellowship as a whole teaching is not just given from the pulpit and left at that. It is given to be worked out, and to be seen to be worked out.

True *ekklesia* teaching, or *koinonia* teaching, then, is never mere theology or theory.

Here's an example. Let's say we're teaching about God's character, and the promises which, because of his character, he has made, promises consequent on his very nature.

One of the attributes of God is that he is 'Jehovah Jireh'—*Provider*. People are not just told that this is what he is, and what he does—so that they all wait passively expecting God to provide for their own or their brother's need. He's a supernatural God, yes. But he also works through very natural means. Members of the fellowship learn practically how God provides through members of Christ's body.

13. Provision

When you read in Philippians: 'My God will supply all your need,' what needs do you think of? Material? Monetary? You would be right, in the context of this verse. It follows immediately after a clear reference to financial supply: 'I am amply supplied, having received from Epaphroditus what you have sent.'

Paul trusted for personal financial supply, and God answered him. He was 'amply supplied.'

But how? From heaven direct? Dropped from the clouds?

God could, of course, do just this. Lonely Elijah was fed by ravens dropping food from the sky. No one is denying that God can and sometimes does provide materially through miracles. Jesus told Peter to obtain their temple tax (equivalent to two days' wages) from the mouth of a fish.

But this wasn't Jesus' normal way, nor is it God's.

In 2 Corinthians 8 and 9 Paul writes of financial provision from members of the body. The Macedonian churches, he says, begged him 'with much entreaty for the favour of participation [*koinonia*] in the support of the saints.' A little further on he describes this support or supply as the 'ministry of this service'. In the early church, we read, there 'was not a needy person among them.'

In our experience this sort of provision is best worked

out in a local home fellowship. Without necessarily living under one roof, or having literally a common purse, we are yet finding out more and more that there need not be anyone in the group seriously in want.

New members—whether by conversion or transfer from other places—often find this a special surprise and joy.

Take the example of Rod and Jean. They became Christians because of the life and example of their neighbours. Before long they began to merge with the local group.

It soon became evident, however, that their finances were all awry, with almost intolerable hire purchase and other debts.

A gift to pay off some of these would by itself not necessarily have helped them in the long run. What they needed was gentle but firm direction on reduced spending, not going into debt, minimizing credit-card use, wise shopping around and the best use of their time. They sought this kind of direction from their leaders. In short, for the first time they began to learn how to exercise care and restraint in stabilizing their budget.

It was all very practical and far-reaching.

Rod was encouraged and helped to find another job, which paid better and was nearer to home. Jean was found to have skills which, when the children were all at school, she could put to use to add to the family income and pay off debts. At the same time the leaders and members of her home group saw to it that none of this detracted significantly from her normal housewife's responsibilities or the time spent with the growing children.

To this family, correction—or, more accurately, restoration—in the area of family finances was a very important part of *salvation*—the soundness and wholeness that God planned for them. The help given was not interference, nor was it 'charity'. It was a welcomed adjustment and of course it was also a discipline. A very necessary one, to enable them to live a fruitful, anxiety-free Christian life.

This didn't all happen without some pain. Rod and Jean needed prodding from time to time. Had you thought of *prodding, stirring* as part of salvation?

14. Stirring

Timothy, one of Paul's 'true sons in the faith', was apparently rather timid. So Paul urged him to 'stir up' or 'kindle afresh' the 'gift of God' which was in him. Although Timothy was here urged to bestir himself, Paul was obviously helping in the process. 'God hasn't given you a spirit of timidity, Timothy,' he said in effect—'but one of power and love and discipline.'

A notable feature of home cells is this giving and receiving of such stimulation. We read of this in Hebrews 10:24: 'Let us consider how to stimulate one another to love and good deeds.' We cannot always rely on some kind of private, spiritual goad to bring us constant reminders of God's specific will for us. The phrase just quoted is 'stimulate *one another*...' (Notice how frequently in the New Testament the words *one another* occur.)

Nor can stimulation be universal or constant in a large congregation. More reserved people can easily be overlooked.

Timothy's weakness—timidity—is very common, isn't it, in church members. Within the smaller grouping shy or reserved people can be gradually and gently drawn out.

So stimulation or prodding is important. It's sometimes unpleasant. But it is more than offset by the security people experience in home cells.

15. Security

Let us never underestimate *refuge* as a major part of salvation. In the midst of deterioration and evil all around us, God is 'our refuge and strength'.

Peter describes salvation as 'escaping the corruption that is in the world through lust.' While we repudiate the idea of escaping from reality, from real life, we don't underrate the seductive and destructive power of Satan and the world around us. We need refuge; we need security.

What practical, down-to-earth, relevant provision has God made for this?

The Psalmist promises: 'He shall cover you with His pinions (outer, flight feathers) and under His wings you may seek refuge.' How are these pinions and wings made real to us? Again we find the answer in people, in the body.

I think David, seven hundred years before Christ and his church, had some idea of this ministry of his fellow believers—refuge, protection, comfort and security. In a magnificent psalm he sings: 'As for the saints who are in the earth, they are the majestic ones in whom is all my delight' (Ps 16:3).

When he says: 'One thing I have asked from the Lord ... that I may dwell in the house of the Lord all the days of my life ... For in the day of trouble He will conceal me in

His shelter...He will hide me,' he could not just have been thinking of the woven tent he had set up on Mount Zion. I believe the Holy Spirit had partially revealed to this man of God, this prophet, as he is often called, the connotation of 'God's house' which we now know.

In Hebrews 3:6 we, God's people, are called his house, and he provides this house for our security. Outside this house we cannot find the same safety.

I cannot help thinking here of the maxim that an Englishman's home is his castle. But no Englishman, nor anyone else for that matter, finds security for his body, soul or spirit in a stone or bricks-and-mortar dwelling.

Safety, security, wholeness—these are all components of *soteria*, salvation. They describe a full-orbed welfare of the whole person, body, soul and spirit. And not only the welfare of the individual, but a soundness and security also in family and corporate life.

We are seeing here, through the ever-growing inter-relationship of local home fellowship members in day-to-day contact, serving one another, gathering and worshipping together, the following fruits of security:

Restoration in marriages

We have not seen any divorces taking place in the ten years or more since home cell division has become an established norm. Marriage and family life, recognized as the foundation of any successful community, receive special attention.

Restoration in family order

God has laid down crystal clear direction concerning the order in a home. 'Christ is the head of every man, and the man is the head of a woman, and God is the head of

Christ.' It must be emphasized that this headship of man, coupled as it is with the headship of Christ and God, is immeasurably sacred and awesome. It is being 'head' God's way. The way the father loved and cared for his only Son. So we teach the divine order in a home, and the right kind of authority, not authoritarianism.

Restoration in finances

This has already been touched on. Finances as such are not usually discussed in the cell gatherings, but consistent contact with other people whose lives are open to counsel tends to further one's desire for this kind of restoration.

Job, housing, future prospects

All these practical details are within the compass of God's care and concern for us. So usually there is provision here too, through the co-operation and help of fellow-members. This leads to further security. It is yet another aspect of salvation.

Spheres of Christian service, personality fulfilment

Through getting to know people well, a leader can be in a better position to discern appropriate avenues of service for each one. For a Christian this is often a vital part of the fulfilment of his personality.

To take simple examples: musical abilities which could pass unnoticed in congregational praise and worship become evident in the home cell situation. A person might unexpectedly display considerable writing skill, or a bent for drama, or even a prophetic gift. Wise leaders try to ensure that these talents are employed in the fellowship gatherings.

This recognition often results in an unprecedented flowering of personality, which in its turn engenders increased personal security.

Health and healing

In Exodus 23:25 we read that God promises conditionally to 'renew sickness' from their midst. In other covenant promise passages in Exodus and Deuteronomy God promises 'none of the diseases' which the Egyptians had—for 'I, the Lord am your healer,' he says. These 'diseases of Egypt' are described in Deuteronomy 28:59 and 60: 'severe and lasting plagues...miserable and chronic sicknesses.'

Old Testament promises, you say. But these are the covenant promises of our God who never changes. We in the New Covenant era 'inherit the promises,' and there is no reason to suppose that God now is any less our 'healer'.

We are in fact beginning to realize, with wonder, something of the reality of these wonderful promises in the local body of Christ, as all members integrate more and more with one another.

That is not to say that there are never accidents, or sickness or death (which comes to everyone) in a community such as this. Much imperfection and weakness there is, of course. But increasingly we are experiencing generally what we may call a 'mantle of health' with many healings and hardly any serious diseases.

The immediacy of prayer and care in each home cell group of the larger congregation is a continual weapon against sickness. Once again God blesses—in this case, heals—through the mediation of his people. When serious illness does strike—rarely—the sense of security and protection actually becomes stronger because all rally to the help of the suffering individual or family. 'When one member suffers, all members suffer,' writes Paul.

We had a striking example of this a few years ago. A gifted young music teacher from a local primary school had contracted leukaemia in the summer of 1977. About six months later, after several weeks of discussions with Christians, he attended a Christmas presentation which was distinctly evangelistic. A few days later Peter and his young wife gave their hearts over to Jesus Christ as their Lord and Saviour. Although medically Peter was incurably ill, his new-found faith and obedience to God consistently grew from this time.

Naturally the church prayed much for him and many of us believed that he would be healed. In new ways the whole body was drawn together by a common concern for Peter and for his healing. This concern was particularly focused through the local home fellowship of which Peter and Ange became members very quickly. The couple often testified that they had never before dreamt of such love, care and help. Despair turned into hope. Darkness into light.

Yet, in October 1978, Peter died, quietly and without great suffering. By now both he and Ange were totally ready for such an eventuality, although to the end we all hoped and prayed for a miraculous recovery.

At the same time we had all felt that the Lord Jesus, who holds the 'keys of death', was sovereign, and would do just what was best for all concerned in the face of this evil disease.

So when death came, Ange had lost all fear of it, all horror. There was no sting. The comfort, strength, and peace of God which he imparted directly, and which was mediated to her through the members of Christ's body, sustained her in a beautiful way. She was more secure than she had ever been, notwithstanding the natural grief at losing her husband.

With reference to this kind of security in the areas outlined above, let us be quite certain of this: God doesn't want us to remain deficient in these areas, to continue year after year with unresolved problems festering like incurable ulcers.

It is true that God can use suffering for our good. But to deduce because of this that God wills us to suffer constantly, especially in the areas outlined above, is wrong. God is on our side. God is for us. His every wish for those who love him is for their well-being, their soundness, their wholeness. This was one reason why Jesus died.

> The chastening for our well-being fell upon Him (Jesus),
> And by His scourging, we are healed.

Jesus suffered in the intensity of Gethsemane and the cross more than any other man, bearing the world's sin in his own body. But he didn't suffer during his life from abject poverty, or ill health, for example. Admittedly he didn't have much housing security, but that was by choice.

Unlike the foxes, he *chose* to have nowhere to lay his head. But he was never insecure. His was a life of 'joy above His fellows,' a life of serenity and security without any fear. In the numerous chapters of the Bible where God's covenant promises are set out for us and where restoration is specifically described, it is abundantly clear that God wants to bless us with a serene, relaxed lifestyle —a lifestyle of wholeness supremely exemplified by Jesus himself.

He didn't depend for this on wealth, or comfort, but nevertheless every need was met and his, I repeat, was a life relaxed, victorious, whole and secure.

Most of us have yet to discover not only the potential of this kind of life as God's norm for us, but the actual experiencing of it year after year.

It is not, of course, a uniformly rosy path—no troubles and a magic Midas-like prosperity. 'Join our fellowship, be a real part of God's *koinonia,* and all your troubles will immediately vanish.' No! But the Bible does hold out the prospect of 'no anxiety', a 'peace that passes comprehension', a provision far greater than that given to birds or flowers, and a 'tranquil and quiet life in all godliness and dignity.'

In a memorable passage, Paul prays for the Colossian Christians that they might be 'God-pleasers: fruitbearing, increasing in knowledge, strong, steadfast, patient, joyful, always giving thanks...' In a word, he sums up, 'sharing in the inheritance of the saints in light.'

This, Paul explains, is possible because God has delivered us from the domain or authority of darkness and transferred us to the kingdom—the kingship, the government—of the Son of his love (Col 1:13).

At the risk of being repetitive I want to stress that I am writing of what we are seeing happening; particularly through the *koinonia* of men, women and children in home fellowship groups. We, and you, can participate *now* in this wonderful inheritance.

16. Leadership

Emerging

There is nothing comparable to the small cell group for ensuring constant personal fulfilment. Many people too diffident to pray, testify, or take part in a large service can find their tongues much more easily in a group of fifteen or so.

Each cell, moreover, becomes a kind of mini-church within the wider local church. Therefore all sorts of ministries such as visiting the sick, collection of tithes and offerings, exposition of Bible themes and the use of the Holy Spirit's gifts can be developed in the small local sphere. Latent talents, which we all have, are brought out in each to a degree quite impossible in a large congregation.

For the successful running of each home cell a good leader is essential. Democracy is not the ideal.

In every home cell there should be a leader raised up by God. We will be looking more closely at the qualities of such a leader in the next chapter. The point here is that the proliferation of home fellowships in a congregation means the proliferation of leaders and assistant leaders.

This is a wonderful opportunity for developing the latent qualities in people in a church. Indeed, it is one of the most satisfying features of cell subdivision. We find that fresh life and leadership emerges from the ranks all the time and people have the opportunity for fulfilment right where they are. Too often people in churches have to seek fulfilment in other organizations—albeit Christian —or be ignored or wasted.

I can think of many examples. In one of our home groups the leader had to relinquish his responsibilities because of circumstances which need not be outlined here. The leaders of the church, having discussed it with the local membership, decided that a certain young family man in the group should take over. He would be under the watchful supervision of an older leader.

But the man chosen genuinely felt he did not have the qualities of leadership. Like Moses, or Jeremiah, he tried to back off. Nevertheless, although up to that time no one had envisaged him as a leader, a man qualified to 'shepherd' the group, we felt he was God's man for the situation. So he accepted the position while still retaining his normal secular employment.

Time has proved him to be the right choice. The fellowship has grown and been consolidated under this man's overall government. He has matured immeasurably and shown considerable wisdom in handling the cell group. His own life, spiritually, and in his family and employment, has much improved.

In the more traditional Western church structure this man could undoubtedly have continued just as a 'member', without realizing leadership capabilities which two years previously were totally hidden, even from himself.

Home cell leaders

When in a previous chapter we looked at Moses' recognition of the basic unit of ten people, the noteworthy feature was that each of these estimated 60,000 small groups had an appointed leader. We read that each man was chosen because he was 'able', 'feared God', and was a 'man of truth' who could 'judge' or lead his group (Ex 18:21).

Many house fellowships have failed through lack of such leadership. Seven years ago I helped to establish one such group in an overseas mission setting, in a developing country. Each member was an earnest Christian, and each had experienced a visitation of the Holy Spirit. But after two years the cell fellowship failed.

Why? Because there was no defined authority. For one thing, the group met without any specific direction from the local church. There was no delegation of leadership or of responsibility by elders or leaders in the local body of Christ. It became a sort of charismatic merry-go-round. When problems arose, there was no final authority to turn to.

So, to have a successful home cell, it is not enough to have a group of enthusiastic people, renewed in the Spirit, meeting together to pray, praise, learn and share—on a democratic basis.

Democracy is not a biblical concept. It was not God's idea, it was Plato's, in the fifth century before Christ!

Throughout scriptural history God ruled by 'delegated authority'. Whenever he wanted a group of called-out people, an *ekklesia*, to hear what he wanted, he found a man and spoke through him. For example, in commissioning Moses and Aaron to go back and free the Israelites, God said to Moses:

> ...he (Aaron) shall speak for you to the people; and it shall come about that he shall be as a mouth for you, and you shall be as God to Him.

So Paul, following this divine principle, tells Timothy to take the things that he, Paul, has taught him and entrust them 'to faithful men who will be able to teach others also.'

When Paul asks his Thessalonian readers to encourage and build up one another, he further charges them to know or appreciate those who diligently labour among them, and 'have charge over' them in the Lord.

The writer to the Hebrews is even more direct: 'Obey your leaders and submit to them, for they keep watch over your souls as those who will give an account' (Heb 13:17).

It is manifestly impossible for a man—for example a sole pastor or priest in a congregation—to 'keep watch' effectively over the souls of say 100 people or more unless he delegates responsibility and authority. So leaders, raised up by God and appointed by the leaders of the whole church, are essential for each home cell.

Leaders led

The key is, I repeat, *delegated* authority. No one arrogates this position to himself (see Heb 5:4). In God's plan there is no place for the self-appointed leader. Even if a man were starting to build a local church congregation with a few foundation members, the project would be devoid of permanent divine blessing unless the man were appointed by God.

In the case of home cell leaders, no one should use his position to build, as we say, his own 'little kingdom'.

Titus, in Crete, is charged by Paul to 'appoint elders in every city,' and Paul, with Barnabas, is recorded as 'appointing elders for the disciples...in every church' (Acts 14:23). It seems obvious that these leaders were local men chosen from among their own people. It must have been the same with Moses' appointment of group leaders.

In our practice here we have found that home fellowship leaders are men clearly raised up by God in the immediate geographical area of the cell group, and acceptable generally to the people they lead. But a most important factor in all these ancient and modern situations is that each leader must himself be led. Or, to put it another way, anyone who would exercise effectively God's authority must himself be under authority.

One of the clearest expositions of this principle is given in Matthew 8. A Roman centurion wanted Jesus to heal his servant, but did not consider himself worthy to have Jesus actually come to his home. 'Just say the word, Jesus,' he said in effect, 'and my servant will be healed.' 'For I too,' he said, 'am a man *under* authority.' The 'too' implied that he recognized that Jesus was under authority as he himself was under the authority of the one who was immediately over him. It was only because he was under authority that he could say to his soldiers 'Go!' or 'Come!' and expect them to obey.

Jesus 'marvelled' at this insight and commended the Roman in glowing terms.

Furthermore, Jesus often affirmed with great emphasis ('truly, truly...') that he acted solely *under* the authority of Another, namely his Father (Jn 5:19 and 30; 8:38; 12:49).

If only every so-called Spirit-renewed leader of cells or fellowships around the world would recognize this principle and willingly work to this rule, a lot of trouble would be avoided. The Scriptures specifically speak against a domineering authority.

To be under another's authority is one of the best safeguards against unscriptural authoritarianism. Being humble, not selfishly motivated, and under the leadership and counsel of other leaders in the church is perhaps the major quality of an effective home cell leader.

There are other important qualities, of course, and I outline some of them next.

Leadership qualities

As well as being humble and teachable, a good leader should be 'above reproach' in his personal life. This doesn't imply perfection, but any current and publicly known unrighteousness bars a man from leading a group.

His marriage, if he is married (neither Jesus nor Paul were), and his family life should set a good example. For the particular task of leading a mixed home fellowship, we have found that it is wise to have married men. The wife stands by her husband and helps him whenever possible, especially if he needs to do what few men can—understand women!

Furthermore, a good home fellowship leader should have the heart of a shepherd, that is, a caring, sensitive heart for people. He should never be concerned merely for programmes, progress or status. Having said this, however, it is still true that the successful leader will be a man with ability to plan and direct imaginatively.

The leader appointed by God should be a man of prayer and one 'apt to teach', that is, ready to counsel and show God's way to people. For this reason he should be a man who reads and knows his Bible, and who is capable of hearing God.

There are other qualities which you will probably think of, especially if you are a leader. A few more of these will be mentioned in chapters on practical hints and avoiding pitfalls.

LOVE will be the prime catalyst of all effective home fellowship leadership. In fact Jesus describes the kind of love and friendship required as that of a man who is willing to lay down his life for others. Love and relationships, we are finding, come before all else.

17. Relationships First

No plans or programmes, skill or status, ideas or ideals will have lasting value in a home cell established by God unless love is there. The kind of love that is 'poured out within our hearts through the Holy Spirit who was given for us.'

'We know that we have passed out of death into life,' writes John.

How do we know? Because we have 'made a decision for Christ'? Because we 'believe in Jesus'?

John could have said these things. But what he writes is: *'because we love the brethren.'*

Quite clearly this is not a mere soulish love like much that passes for love in the world around us. Nor is it merely an expressed 'love for all God's people.'

Years ago I occasionally used to search my heart to see if there was any hate there—anyone whom I hated. Then, if I could not find any, I concluded that I had love for all God's people. A mere absence of hate! I believe now that this was to me, and countless others, a deception from the Evil One.

When we read in Colossians that love is the 'perfect bond of unity', we are reading of something positive and real. This kind of bond, this kind of love is made up of practical, day-by-day attitudes and acts toward and within a group of people small enough in numbers to make that love real.

Jesus, in that prayer partly quoted earlier, prays to his Father that his small group of disciples 'may be one, just as we are one. I in them and Thou in Me, that they may be perfected in unity,' or as the margin has it, *'into a unit.'*

So, what I am writing about is love expressed in relationships. Holy Spirit-forged relationships. The literal translation of 2 Corinthians 5:14 is: 'The love of Christ *holds* us together.' The Greek word translated *holds* is *sunecho* which means to press together. Love presses us together, an action which could be likened to that of a car clutch. Or, to change the metaphor, the love of Christ is a strong cement binding us together into a unit.

The value of these relationships, however, is not just for those who relate. God has a far wider purpose in it all.

18. Evangelism

I alluded earlier to Martin Luther King's 'I had a dream!' Jesus, too, had a dream, expressed in his celebrated high-priestly prayer in John 17. His disciples would be perfected in unity. For what purpose? Jesus goes on: *'that the world may know...'*

Peter expresses the same purpose in the even wider context of God's choosing of his people:

> You are a chosen race, a royal priesthood, a holy nation, a people for God's own possession.

Why?

> ...that you may proclaim the excellence of Him who has called you out of darkness into His marvellous light.

God's *ekklesia,* his calling out of us, his people, was not just for his pleasure, or for our good, our salvation. It was as a demonstration to the world of what God is like—his excellencies—and what he wants to do for all: call us from darkness into his marvellous light.

I once heard Ern Baxter put it this way:

> We are to be the extension of the society of the Trinity on the earth, to catch the eye of the world. Not of course to have them say, 'What a wonderful people,' but 'What a wonderful

God!' and to be drawn to Him. To want to be part of His community. To be saved!

So here's a home cell group where there is a *sunecho* kind of love between the members, where each stone in the building or 'spiritual house' is 'living', as Peter, again, puts it. Where the direction is divinely delegated, and where the lifestyle of the members is increasingly after God's pattern: free, warm, pure, serene, secure and joyful.

Such a *koinonia* group does not exist for itself. It is a proclamation to the wider community around it—the neighbours, if you like—of God's 'excellencies', his character, his attributes.

It is a lighthouse in a stormy sea. Or, to use another figure, it is an oasis in a desolate wilderness. A lighthouse glows, but it doesn't have to organize a campaign. An oasis beckons by just being there; the greenness and water attract the thirsty desert traveller.

So the home cell group whose lifestyle is displaying attributes of the triune God does not necessarily have to strain to witness or invite others. Such a group has a magnetism all of its own and through such the Lord can 'add to the church daily such as would be saved.'

We are beginning to realize that the effective *living* of these small groups of people in their natural local neighbourhoods is one of God's principal means of evangelism in this day and age.

All around, at least in the Western world, we see decay and deterioration in society's foundations. Broken marriages, couples living together unmarried, broken homes, delinquent children, drug addiction, suicides and increasing crime. When people in these situations see the wholeness, peace, purity and zest of a group of ordinary people relating together with what is to the world abnormal enjoyment and love, there is often a wistful longing to know how this comes about, and who brought it about.

Was Paul thinking of this, at least partly, when he wrote:

That the manifold wisdom of God might now be made known *through the church*...?

It is in their neighbourhood setting, as much as on a wider scale, that God is planning 'the revealing of the sons of God,' which 'the whole creation is *standing on tiptoe*' waiting to see (Rom 8:19, J. B. Phillips' translation).

Surely, in these days, God's dream is many thousands of *restoration* churches around the globe, made up of myriads of cells, small *koinonia*, Holy Spirit-filled groups of Jesus' love-knit-together people, living as God's society, his alternative society in the world.

This is God's *now* strategy for evangelism. One thing is certain in what the Spirit is saying to the churches these days: *koinonia*, not *institution*, to win the world. (See Appendix for a tabulated comparision between the two.)

19. War!

There is no such thing as a one-man army. We as Christians are engaged in constant warfare and we cannot make it alone. For too long we have looked at spiritual warfare as being a sort of individual hand-to-hand combat, a lone battle.

Take the well-known verses in Ephesians 6:

> Put on the whole armour of God...for our struggle is not against flesh and blood but against the rulers, against the powers, against the world forces of this darkness, against the spiritual forces of wickedness in the heavenly places.

What an enemy! And this is not Pauline hyperbole.

The key to the taking up of armour and the battle is missed somewhat in English where a verb such as *'put on'* is the same spoken to one or spoken to a group, and where *'you'* is singular or plural. Every verb and pronoun in this Ephesian passage is plural, corporate: take up, be able to resist, stand firm, gird loins. 'All of you, as a body, put on the full armour of God,' is what Paul is saying.

It is not 'my struggle is not against flesh and blood,' but *'our* struggle.'

If there is any realm in which we need one another in the body, it is the war against Satan. The most telling illustration of this is surely provided by our own bodies. When a germ-laden thorn pierces my finger, the finger

does not fight alone against the alien attack. Hosts of
antibodies in my blood from all over my body rally to the
fray against poison and infection. My tongue and my
other hand also assist in the battle.

So in the body of Christ we, its members, stand together
against the enemy. It happens most easily and effectively
in the house group.

During a period, say, of weeks John has a bout of
depression; Maureen finds it hard to forgive her mother-
in-law; Jill and Jeff have reached a low in their marriage;
Adrian is very angry about the increased show of porn-
ography in his local newsagent's shop; Robert's adult son
has temporarily left the fellowship and is having a very
hard struggle; Debbie is finding it very hard to give up a
boyfriend who is not a Christian and whose principles are
definitely anti-God; Frank and Barbara are concerned
about the subtle teaching their two children are receiving
in their school, throwing doubt on the Bible and standards
of righteousness.

What a relief for each one to be able to share with the
others in the cell family and for them all to be able to stand
together against the devil in the various guises he assumes!

So the home cell is both a fortress for defence and a
battle station for attack. The armour and weapons to be
employed corporately and individually are set out in
Ephesians 6 and elsewhere—e.g. the shield of faith, the
sword of the Spirit, and above all, prayer and petition 'at
all times'.

20. Preparation

Although there is spontaneity and relaxation in home cell gatherings, it should not be thought that they do not require any preparation. Ideally, for maximum success of any meeting or project, all should prepare to some degree.

But in this brief chapter I will be touching mainly on the preparation plans and prayer of the leader.

A. W. Tozer has pointed out a general truth that is both simple and profound. He says in effect that anything we do which is self-initiated and which stems merely from our own thinking has no permanence in the kingdom of God. By contrast, whatever we do, if it is Holy-Spirit-initiated and directed, will have permanent results in God's plans and economy.

So the secret of planning for an evening or a series of evenings with one's home cell members is waiting on God. That is, to enquire of him what he wants and to learn to hear and rely on what the Holy Spirit directs.

This means that the lines of communication between a leader and his God must be kept open. It is not necessarily difficult; God has made it gloriously possible for us to know his will and to delight in it.

But it takes a sacrifice of time and effort. The overall leader can delegate to others in the group, frequently if possible. But such details as the main theme each time, the nature of each gathering, the involvement of others—who and when—in actual ministry, the ensuring of freshness and variety as the weeks go on, the sensitivity to varying needs of different ones—all these mean careful and prayerful planning.

A good leader is a creative man. When all is said and done, we all have creative potential, being made in the image of the Creator. Nothing is more likely to kill the sense of expectation and delight which should mark the group's getting together and sameness and dullness.

Over the years here we have compiled a couple of lists: one of practical suggestions of different forms cell meetings can take, and activities and projects; the other of various ways the members can participate.

There is a certain amount of overlapping in these two, naturally, but I offer them in the next two chapters in the hope that they will be read and used—and added to in each local situation.

21. Home Cell Evenings—
Thirty Suggestions

'Et nova et vetera' (things new and old) was the motto of a theological seminary I once attended. The words came from a question and answer session Jesus had with his disciples in a house, after he had preached to 'great multitudes' on a beach. He said to the disciples:

> Every scribe who has become a disciple of the Kingdom of heaven is like a head of a household, who brings forth out of his treasure things new and old.

It is good to have a treasure or small store-house of ideas and suggestions. This does not preclude the Holy Spirit's prompting. He never set a premium on poverty of ideas or imagination.

So here are some thirty suggestions as to ways of running home cell gatherings. (I want to avoid using the term 'meetings', because one thing this book shows, I hope, is that home cells consist of people interacting and relating, rather than merely attending meetings.)

The suggestions are set out in the form of brief notes and they are given as a stimulus. They are just a start, to be added to. No special order of importance has been attempted, but I've tended to commence with the more orthodox and well-known ideas and move on to others perhaps less familiar.

If you find any that seem to you unsuitable, just don't use them. But please note that all of these have been tried, over the years, and have not been found wanting. In each case the idea given is like a main theme or emphasis. Many meetings will use more than one of these suggestions.

1. Bible study by a leader or visiting speaker. All encouraged to take notes. Preferably followed by some discussion.

2. Bible study by a selected group member or members. I heard an excellent and very practical one by two young single women on 'Hospitality'.

3. Planned question-and-answer session to expand on Bible teaching given on Sunday.

4. Testimony evening—say, at a year's end. Each participant to be informed beforehand. No compulsion! Up-to-date testimonies—not just what God did for you twenty years ago!

5. Special prayer night for special needs, such as healing. (By no means does this imply that prayer would not be appropriate and natural on nearly every occasion.)

6. A coming together after a day or days of fasting, to share any revelation, to pray together and perhaps to come against Satan in the matter which prompted the fast.

7. Bible and/or Fellowship Quiz. By the latter I mean something to 'get to know the members of your "family" better.'

8. A meal together, followed perhaps by Communion. 'After supper he took the cup...'

9. A music night. Bring in an expert from the church to introduce more part-singing to the group.

10. A Christian music records and tapes evening. Planned and with purpose, interspersed by comments.

11. A craft evening. All working and learning together; something new but not too hard, e.g. simple pottery.

12. A carefully planned games evening with perhaps the special aim of learning more about one another—or just to have fun together.

13. Break up into pairs or small groups for discussion, intercession or planning. Pool the findings at the end.

14. A weekend away together. When we do this, the aim usually is informality and relaxation. Perhaps some ministry as well.

15. An evening to plan a special outreach venture, e.g. an Easter presentation in a local hall, with an evangelistic emphasis.

16. The outreach itself. It could be an effective demonstration of living and relating together—through, say, drama and testimony.

17. While the operation of the gifts of the Spirit should be often in evidence at meetings, it is a good idea to have an occasional evening when these are specifically explained and encouraged—gifts such as tongues, prophecy, etc.

18. A writing evening. Don't necessarily inform beforehand. Distribute paper and pencils. Urge each one to express him or herself freely. Suggest prose, prayers, poetry or praise. Remember poetry does not necessarily have rhyme or rhythm.

19. An excerpt evening. Each prepares beforehand. Bring excerpts from books, newspapers, magazines which have helped (or warned!) the reader.

20. A serving evening. Each one goes out of his way to serve, help, prefer or honour another or others.

21. Entertain another home group as guests for the evening. Purely social, or a combination of social and shared worship and ministry.

22. Go out for a social time together—on the regular evening, or on a Saturday perhaps: boating, skating, open air sports, walking etc.

23. Invite neighbours along to an informal evening or day together.

24. A 'Psalm' evening—members read out biblical psalms or psalm-poems they have written themselves.

25. Special missionary evening—either with a visiting speaker or to learn and pray.

26. A book evening—led by a Christian bookshop manager or salesman, with lots of good books.

27. A drama night. Acting out church situations; preparing small dramatic sketches to illustrate kingdom truths. One of the best I have seen was by four young people who in twenty minutes prepared a 'puppet' (hand in blanket) sketch on the theme: 'The ability to take correction is a sign of maturity.'

28. Interpretation of scripture choruses by mime or movement. Perhaps then share with the wider congregation at a regular service.

29. An evening, afternoon or day of serving or helping a needy person, family or group, decorating, cooking, mending—or even taking on an outing.

30. Various kinds of verbal sharing evenings—by members or visitors; what God has done for me or been to me this week; major difficulties as a Christian.

22. Member Participation

'Julie is part of our group; she attends regularly week by week. But she never opens her mouth.'

Well, all Julie may need are some suggestions about how she can break the ice. It is obvious too that the leader should seek her out and talk to her naturally and gently about her reluctance to take part.

In 'church', Julie could be almost mute for ten years or more, and no one pick it up. But in small group gatherings her very silence speaks. It invites counsel and help.

At any rate, Julie and many others could profit by being presented with a wide variety of ways in which they can participate. A good starting point is 1 Cor 14:26.

> When you assemble, each one has a psalm, has a teaching, has a revelation, has a tongue, has an interpretation...

Each one of these categories can be expanded, so here is a list of suggestions. 'You' are the reader, and an actual or prospective home cell member.

Psalm

1. Suggest a hymn or scripture chorus or two.
2. Read a psalm which includes verses set to music. The reading is followed by all singing these.

3. Read out a poem or written expression of praise which you have written.

4. Suggest and help in the group's attempt to put a verse (or verses previously selected) to simple music.

5. Offer to sing a psalm or song which you've heard or composed.

Teaching

6. Read out a selected scripture passage.

7. Give brief thoughts on a short scripture passage.

8. Having pre-arranged it, give a Bible study on a selected theme.

Revelation

9. Give thoughts on a word or verse which has come alive to you during the week.

10. Give a prophecy, that is, what you feel God is speaking into a current situation. We suggest such being given in natural language, not in Shakespearean English peppered with 'yea' and other obsolete words.

11. Speak a word of wisdom or knowledge (two of the promised Spirit's gifts; Gk *charismata*) into a situation or problem, if God gives these. This can be done during a time of prayer or worship, or during a discussion.

Tongue

12. Give a spoken tongue, and if no interpretation is forthcoming, don't worry. Pray for it yourself. (See 1 Cor 14:13.)

13. Sing in a tongue. This is often a good way to get started in public utterance. Many people find it easier to sing than speak in a tongue.

Interpretation

14. Interpret a spoken tongue. Remember, an interpretation isn't a translation. Learn to wait on God for this and expect sometimes to be given it.

15. Interpret a tongue which has been sung. This may be in singing to the same or similar melody, or it may be spoken.

Other ways

16. Pray—including thanksgiving, adoration, petition or intercession. Brief, natural prayer—like a child to a father. God does not need doctrinal dissertations!

17. Ask for prayer for some personal need or problem.

18. Suggest group prayer for some local or national issue.

19. Prepare a small mime or sketch beforehand. For example: 'We'd like to illustrate "Do all things without murmuring" by the following mime (or sketch).'

   This sort of thing can bring great blessing and even revelation to others. Moreover the use of mime and drama opens up a large field of variety in meetings.

20. If you are so moved, 'dance before the Lord' as David did. This could be spontaneous or prepared. A lot, of course, will depend on the room in which you gather.

21. Use a solo instrument to bless others—say, a cello, or a flute. In David's era instruments were invariably used for praise.

22. Suggest ways of helping or serving others in the local or wider fellowship.

23. Arrange beforehand and present a duet or trio or small singing group. Not as a mere 'item', but to bring light, revelation or encouragement to others.

24. Teach a new chorus or hymn which you have learnt.

25. Bring, by yourself or with others, questions to the group's leader(s). But never let a home cell gathering develop into a mere academic discussion or long theological debate.

26. Read a pertinent excerpt from a newspaper, magazine or book, either secular or Christian. Discuss.

27. Use visual art forms to teach or show something: for example, a drawing, a painting or sculpture which you have made yourself. I have seen artistically constructed banners used to bless others.

28. Pray for another with laying on of hands. The Bible counsels to 'pray for one another that you may be healed.'

29. Do something special as appreciation for, or honour to, your leader. I quote from 1 Thessalonians 5:11–12: 'We request of you, brethren, that you appreciate those who diligently labour among you, and have charge over you in the Lord and give you instruction, and that you esteem them very highly in love because of their work.'

Here is a word of counsel for every member, anywhere.

Be prepared through prayer and creative planning to participate on any occasion when God may want you to. Don't be content to let others do it all. By the same token, you bolder ones, give others a chance!

23. Pitfalls

This is a brief chapter on some of the mistakes which can not only hinder growth of a cell group, but may even kill it.

Cliques

All must be of one mind. Two or more members getting together and displaying bias or favouritism will soon undermine true *koinonia*. If this develops further and leads to gossip or slander the outcome will often be tragedy. In the kingdom of God, that is, where Jesus governs, there is no place for judgement, malice or destructive criticism.

Little Kingdoms

Each cell is an integral part of the whole congregation. Power can corrupt, as we all know. The authority God wants leaders to have in his body is never possessive or selfish. There is always a danger that success in a group can go to the leader's head and he can be tempted to grasp it to himself and for his own advantage and build, as we say, a 'little kingdom' for himself. Members also can do this and plead collectively that they are a special group needing special status or privileges.

Domination

Even if he had no desire to build his own little kingdom, a leader with abilities well beyond those of his members can excessively dominate his group. Quite often the best leader will 'direct from the wings' and will delegate a great deal of responsibility in order to develop the potential of those under his care.

It is valuable here to remind ourselves of Jesus' words:

> You know that the rulers of the Gentiles lord it over them, and their great men exercise authority over them. It is not so among you, but whoever wishes to become great among you shall be your servant, and whoever wishes to be first among you shall be your slave; just as the Son of Man did not come to be served, but to serve, and to give His life a ransom for many.

Rebels

Groups can be much hindered by rebels in their midst.

Let me explain this, because 'rebels' sounds a hard word.

I have already written of the overall need for *love* in all home cell operation. But love in the scriptural sense is not weakness, universal tolerance, or indulgence. Surely we recognize that Jesus supremely exemplified love, but he could be very intolerant with certain people. Especially religious people such as many Pharisees and scribes. Jesus condemned these outright:

> You travel about on sea and land to make one proselyte; and when be becomes one, you make him twice as much a son of hell as yourselves.

And these Pharisees considered that they were part of God's chosen people!

So if there is someone in your home cell group who constantly fails to be in harmony with the rest, or who month after month cannot agree with the general direction of the group and the church, the leader must take action.

The leader's responsibility is to protect the whole group. So he should speak to the offending one before real damage is done and, following the procedure set out in Matthew 18:15–18, attempt to persuade him to co-operate. If the person remains obdurate, he or she must be asked not to attend.

Occasionally a rebel can be one who is deliberately infiltrated by people wanting to destroy the cell. If the leader is appointed and anointed by God, and sensitive to all that promotes the welfare of the whole cell, he will soon discern the danger and take firm action.

We shall be considering in the last chapter ways to establish the group in such a way that this kind of rebellion does not often occur, if at all.

Extroverts

Beware of members or adherents who, although not leaders, always seem to want to dominate in participation. I am referring here not to rebels, but to people who are often well-meaning but do not realize that because they are more extrovert than others they bring about an imbalance in the cell group.

A wise leader can usually handle this, not so much publicly but privately.

Lack of clear objectives

Hopefully this little book will help to provide some clear objectives. Each leader and member should be ever ready to reappraise his goals and motives. God does not want any of his *ekklesia*, be they minuscule cells or large congregations, to be static.

We must know where we're going and have clearly defined goals.

Sameness

I used to have the strange belief that at the dawn of creation God made the universe and man and then, somehow, stopped creating. He continued merely to maintain the whole cosmos.

This of course is not true. Ours is a creative God whose mercies are 'new every morning'. His mind is teeming with millions of wonderful plans for millions of lives. I am certain he never meant life in his kingdom to be boring and dull. He intends it to be fresh, purposeful, challenging. Jesus told his disciples that he had come that they might have life and might have it abundantly.

Variety is said to be the spice of life. Variety is certainly an essential element in the life of a home cell group.

Leaders and members should be constantly aware of the danger of monotony, of getting into a rut. One way of avoiding stagnation is to have frequent emergence of new leadership. Each man tends to put something of his own individual stamp on a group. So we look next at the selection of new leaders and their training.

24. Training Leaders

Timothy was told to entrust the things that he had heard from Paul 'to faithful men who will be able to teach others also.'

The constant discovery and development under God of good, fresh leadership is undoubtedly the main key to successful growth—both in home cells and in the life of the whole church.

Here are nine practical suggestions for leadership training:

Relationships

More important than leaders' meetings, lectures, and training seminars is the development of relationships between leaders, and between leaders and those who lead *them*.

We have a saying in the Fellowship here which expresses a very important truth: 'When the leadership gets it together, the body will get it together.'

We have already noted that Jesus chose to limit his main work of discipling to a small number of men. Jesus was training those men to be leaders themselves; they were the ones who would be discipling others. As he taught them he repeatedly placed emphasis on their relationships with his Father, with him and with one another.

So it is imperative that any house cell leader should give

time and attention to the development of other men in the group as potential leaders, and his first priority will be the building up of warm, friendly relationships, with an emphasis on loyalty and unity.

This is done in many down-to-earth ways, including social activity, sport, fun, as well as in prayer, fellowship, teaching and discussions.

One mind

Unity between leaders or prospective leaders, does not imply a group of servile 'yes men'. Each leader is an individual who has found and knows God for himself. Just as interaction between members in the cell has been stressed, so must there be a maximum interaction between leaders, and his trainees.

By and large there should be unanimity on all major issues. Nevertheless, what is most sought after is not mere unanimity but Spirit-given unity. As stated earlier, theocracy is the ideal, not democracy.

People matter

It must never be forgotten that what we are chiefly concerned about is not structure, plans or programmes, but *people*.

So the leadership training sessions will major on people, the members of the group with their problems and potential. There will be sharing about how to tackle this or that situation. There will often be an attempt together in discussion and prayer to get to the bottom of so-and-so's deep-seated problem. All with love and compassion, not with harsh judgement and complaint.

Motivation

The trainer will always be alert to the attitudes and motivation of his trainees. There should be repeated encouragement to wait on God in order to obtain his mind. Help may need to be given on how to pray, how to find private Bible study interesting and challenging, how to overcome temptation and attain righteousness.

The leader is keeping watch over the souls of these trainees to 'give an account' (Heb 13:17). He must therefore be sensitively and compassionately responsible.

Promotion

I am alluding here to the promotion of each man's best interests in line with his particular gifting—not necessarily a secular type of promotion. Each one should receive appropriate encouragement alongside any correction and warning.

Potential

Care must be taken to ensure development especially in the areas in which each man is gifted. Certainly not every man will have a true 'shepherding' gift. Some may show aptitude more in the realm of organization or in teaching or in the leading of praise and worship.

So the leader must have discernment and wisdom to draw out of each man that for which God has called him. He must be careful not to put square pegs into round holes.

Transparency

In all of the above, truth and honesty—'the truth in love'

—must prevail. Masks must be taken off. Men must be willing to be vulnerable. There must be a continual openness with one another.

It often takes a long time to develop this; especially with men who have been brought up in more traditional church patterns. Hence, again, the need for constant emphasis on developing friendship and mutual trust.

Couples

According to the New Testament, positions of governmental leadership in the church are always to be filled by men. But at the same time the Scriptures speak of a man and his wife as being 'one flesh'. So it is a good idea to have sessions sometimes which get together the leaders and their wives.

Restraint

Need it be said again, the leader must be ready to be firm when he discerns tendencies in a trainee to build his own little kingdom or a self-assertiveness which hinders unity.

Therefore it must be made clear to every would-be leader that God's kind of leader is unselfish, humble and willing to be under leadership and authority himself. He should be taught to recognize the 'beam in his own eye'—such as selfishness or power-grasping—and to welcome correction of such by other men.

These are some practical guidelines. All through, each one must realize that it is the *calling* that is important. It is a 'holy calling', a 'high calling', a 'heavenly calling'. It is awesome, but glorious, and Peter counsels us: 'be diligent to make certain about your calling...'

25. How to Start

As we have seen, home fellowships have sprung up in many parts of the world. But very many churches still resist cellular division. One problem you may have is that the whole prospect of such subdivision is too daunting. 'How would it be possible for this to come about in our church?' you may be asking.

A primary word of advice to you would be—start in simple, natural ways. Don't try to do too much, too soon. If God is in the inauguration he will direct and move to develop and expand it.

Instruction

The first step, clearly, is to *teach* the concepts of discipleship, maturing, relationships, spiritual authority and the need for pastoral care to be given to every individual church member. These principles are expounded and described much more fully in *Built to Last* (Kingsway Publications) which I wrote as a sequel to this book. You cannot just intellectually argue people into accepting these kingdom principles. The Holy Spirit whom Jesus called the Spirit of truth will have to open their hearts and instruct them.

So what you will find is that, after some weeks or months of careful teaching, there will be those who respond and who will be willing to come together in a home group to begin cellular life.

Recognizing leaders

This is the first step. It must come initially from the leadership of the church, and then from the people who will make up the first house cells. Without previous experience there may be some strangeness and nervousness, but if the few who pioneer the subdivision are convinced that it is God's purpose and his timing, faith and hope will soon overcome these.

Site

We are finding here in practice that the leader's own home is the best venue for cell gatherings. However, this does not need to be a hard and fast rule.

Often, an important consideration is one of geography.

In our twenty or so groups in Basingstoke, geography is frequently the deciding factor for each person. That is, there is a defined cell group for the area each one lives in, and he or she joins that group. Since spending time together not only on one night of the week but as often as possible is the goal, geographical proximity is important.

We know, however, of other churches where such a consideration is not practical. John Smith may live twenty miles away from any other member, say on a farm. Mary Jones may wish to attend the fellowship of her fiancé. We have proved more and more, recently, that relationships are more important than geography.

Don't impose

The guiding principle to be adopted is naturalness and

easiness. Don't be rigid or artificial. Don't try to squeeze people into an awkward mould. Let there be general agreement. Don't impose a form on unwilling members.

Furthermore—and this applies to all structural patterns—let there be flexibility before and after you commence. God doesn't fit into any strait-jacket, and we should be open to the Spirit's promptings at all times to change if necessary.

So if the original subdivisions need revising, revise them, after prayer and dialogue. In this connection, local initiative is very important. Don't dictate!

Even as I was writing the above paragraphs this evening a good friend, a pastor from the south-west of Britain, called me on the telephone to report on his fellowship. His church introduced home cells three or four years ago but only last week decided to change their composition quite considerably. After much debate with the elders and leaders they decided to increase the number from five to six groups and to make some changes in the composition of each and in the leadership.

Initial get-togethers

It may help some people if I outline a suggested pattern for the first meeting or two. The aim is to put people at ease, and unite them. When all have gathered in the sitting room, perhaps serve coffee and spend the first half hour in getting people to chat informally together. Then, as music is usually appropriate at the start, sing some hymns and choruses of praise followed by quieter singing which encourages worship and adoration of the Lord.

If some people can pray audibly, encourage this next for, say fifteen minutes; if not, pre-arrange for two or three to pray. Then you may want to read, comment on, and discuss a passage such as 1 Corinthians 12:4–27 or

1 Corinthians 4:26.

This could be followed by an invitation to share special problems (or triumphs!) and prayer requests. Don't force people to speak. Follow with some specific prayer regarding the matters raised.

Towards the end have a brief planning session with everyone, to map out a tentative programme for the next month or two. Remember: aim for variety; keep everything to purpose; delegate tasks to others.

Then in closing, it may be appropriate for all to stand together holding hands, and in silence (or audibly) to commit the new undertaking and one another in a very definite way to God for his direction and presence. Repeat the Grace together.

Re-appraisal

This is necessary from the outset. Each leader should be alert and eager for a good start. Cultivate relationships. Avoid rigidity of programme. Introduce healthy variety early. Be a good listener. Local leaders and overall leaders *must* spend time together (weekly if possible) to hammer out problems and find God's will together, and above all to relate together.

Initial commitment

I have deliberately left this to last. It is vital to establish clear principles of commitment at the beginning. Don't sacrifice these for the sake of numbers, or to accommodate a wide spectrum.

Each member at the outset should know clearly what commitment to the other cell members and the leader means. Each member should verbally declare such commitment in the presence of the eldership, or church leadership, before cells are started. This kind of under-standing before commencement will clear the ground and prevent rebels or dissidents getting in and breaking up fellowship.

There need be no fear that this narrowing-down will ultimately be counter-productive. God isn't interested in quantity at the expense of quality. A very revealing verse in Proverbs reads: 'He who raises his door seeks des-truction' (Prov 17:19).

Jesus' plans to evangelize the world and establish his church depended initially on eleven men. Three thousand were saved at Pentecost, but they were 'added to the church'. When those eleven got it right, and moreover were baptized in the Spirit, the numbers came.

So, to conclude, the whole undertaking must be initiated *by the Spirit* and carried on in his direction and power.

We believe that all the principles set out in these chapters are grounded on the scriptural *restoration* patterns. If this is so, and you start with these foundations, and the Holy Spirit prompts all that you do, you will be assured of success by the head of the church, Jesus Christ himself.

God bless you as you not only hear, but *do*!

Appendix
Koinonia V. Institution

*Characteristics of
Koinonia:*

*Characteristics of
Institution:*

Typified by the tabernacle,
especially David's, on
Mt Zion.

Typified by the temple,
especially Solomon's or
Herod's.

Made up of small units.

A large unit.

Flexible.

Inflexible.

Ready for, and open to,
constant change, both in the
individual and the small groups.

Resistant to change,
especially in the corporate
programme pattern.

Mobile; can spring up freely
wherever appropriate.

Fixed, limited usually to the
building or the organization.

Holy Spirit-led patterns of
structure.

Imposed patterns of structure—
often historical.

Spontaneous Holy Spirit-
prompted worship, praise
and expression.

Traditional patterns of
worship, often printed.

Revelation playing a vital part.

Tradition-led.

Theocratic (rule of God).

Autocratic (rule of one),
democratic (rule of the people)
or oligarchic (rule of few).

Non-professional leadership
(very few house cell leaders
would be seminary trained).

Professional leadership.

Little emphasis if any on the
distinction between ordained
or clerical and 'lay'.

'Clergy' and 'lay' usually
distinct.

Charismatic or Spirit-given
gifts primarily recognized and

Natural gifts primarily
recognized and used

used.

(including, e.g. ability to preach or lead or organize).

'Body ministry'—i.e. all participating (or able to participate) in worship, sharing, etc.

Ministry mainly or only by 'ministers' or special 'lay' assistants.

Growth through new members getting saved— attracted by the lifestyle of existing members.

Growth, if at all, through campaigns and organization.

Simple.

Elaborate.

Multiplication by division— cells dividing to multiply in numbers as people are attracted in.

Multiplication, if any, by new buildings, new campaigns, new staff, new areas and new plans.

Notes

Page Reference

39 ibid. p. 41
ibid. pp. 45-46
J. Taylor Hamilton and
Kenneth E. Hamilton *History
of the Moravian Church*,
Moravian Church in America,
Bethlehem Pa. 1967, p. 24

40 ibid. p. 36
ibid. p. 36
(100 years) A. J. Lewis op.
cit. p. 60 line 19
ibid. p. 56
ibid. p. 22
ibid. p. 22

41 E. C. Kenyon, *Life of John
Wesley*, Walter Scott Ltd.,
London, 1891, p. 151
ibid. p. 28

42 Howard A. Snyder, *The
Problem of Wineskins*, IVP.
Illinois, 1978, p. 140
ibid. p. 139

43 'The church around the world'
Pamphlet Vol. 9 No. 7 June
1979 IVP Illinois
J. W. and K. L Hurston,
'caught in the Web . . . the
Home Cell Unit System,'
Church Growth International,
1977, p. 14
ibid. p. 23
ibid. p. 35
ibid. p. 24 ('from 8-15 units')

44 ibid. p. 24
ibid. p. 67
Renewal magazine No. 60
Dec. 75/Jan. 76.
Fountain Trust, Surrey,
England p. 18

48 Jn 5:39
Mt 6:15 (paraphrased)

51 2 Cor 5:17
Rom 12:2
2 Cor 3:18
Lk 14:27
Mt 3:8

52 Mt 5:20
Gal 6:1–2
Eph 4:16

56 Phil 2:12

57 Eph 3:17–18
1 Jn 4:20

Page Reference

57 Rom 12:5 etc.

60 Is 53:6

61 Ex 18:17
1 Kings 19:18

62 Mt 11:28
1 Pet 5:7
1 Pet 5:3

63 Gal 6:2
Acts 20:28
1 Thess 5:9, 10, 11

64 1 Cor 14:26

66 1 Thess 5:14 ('undisciplined'
margin)
Prov 10:17
Heb 12:11

67 2 Tim 2:24, 25

69 Gal 5:22
Jn 15:16
Jn 15:4
Jn 15:12

70 Gal 5:22

72 Gen 22:14

73 Phil 4:19
Phil 4:18
2 Cor 8:4
2 Cor 9:12
Acts 4:34

76 1 Tim 1:2
2 Tim 1:6–7

77 Ps 46:1
2 Pet 1:4
Ps 91:4
Ps 27:4–5

78 1 Cor 11:3

80 Ex 15:26 and Deut 7:15
Heb 6:12
1 Cor 12:26

81 Rev 1:18

82 Is 53:5
Mt 8:20
Heb 1:9
e.g. Deut 28

83 Phil 4:6 and 7
Mt 6:26f
1 Tim 2:2

86 Ex 4:16
2 Tim 2:2

87 1 Thess 5:12
Titus 1:5

88 Mt 8:8–10
1 Pet 5:3

89 1 Tim 3:2

Page Reference

89	1 Tim 3:4
	1 Tim 3:2 (KJV)
	Jn 15:13
90	Rom 5:5
	1 Jn 3:14
	Col 3:14
91	Jn 17:21–23
92	Jn 17:23
	1 Pet 2:9
93	1 Pet 2:5
	Acts 2:47 (KJV)
94	Eph 3:10
95	Eph 6:11–14
96	Eph 6:18
97	Ps 40:8
99	Mt 13:52
100	1 Cor 11:25
101	1 Cor 14:26
105	Phil 2:14
	2 Sam 6:14

Page Reference

106	1 Chron 15:16–24
	Jas 5:16
109	Mt 20:25–28
	Mt 23:15
111	Lam 3:23
	Jn 10:10
112	2 Tim 2:2
113	1 Pet 3:8
114	1 Pet 5:2
115	Eph 4:15
	Eph 5:31
	Mt 7:3, 4
	holy calling: 2 Tim 1:9
	high calling: Phil 3:14
	heavenly calling: Heb 3:1
	2 Pet 1:10
120	Acts 2:47
	Much of the Appendix kindly supplied by my colleague, Tony Gray, at Basingstoke.

If you wish to contact the author or the church concerned the address is as follows:

Basingstoke Community Church
48 Sarum Hill,
Basingstoke,
Hampshire,
England.

Tel (0256) 55617 or (0256) 23043

Built to Last

by Ron Trudinger

When Ron Trudinger wrote *Cells for Life* many churches were discovering the advantages of subdividing into home groups.

Since then a sequel has become necessary, because there is a real danger of introducing home groups as little more than a church face-lift. If the principles underlying church restoration are not understood, there will be no lasting benefit for the church. 'Restoration' is the necessary return to clear biblical patterns of church structure.

In this book Ron Trudinger (a pastor at Basingstoke Community Church) draws on his experience of restoration church life to apply the Bible's teaching in a direct and practical way.

K
Kingsway Publications